OBSERVATIONS

UPON

THE FLORIDAS.

OBSERVATIONS

UPON

THE FLORIDAS.

BY

CHARLES VIGNOLES,

CIVIL AND TOPOGRAPHICAL ENGINEER.

A FACSIMILE REPRODUCTION

OF THE 1823 EDITION

WITH AN

INTRODUCTION AND INDEX

BY *JOHN HEBRON MOORE.*

BICENTENNIAL FLORIDIANA
FACSIMILE SERIES.

A UNIVERSITY OF FLORIDA BOOK.

THE UNIVERSITY PRESSES OF FLORIDA.

GAINESVILLE 1977.

THE BICENTENNIAL FLORIDIANA
FACSIMILE SERIES
published under the sponsorship of the
BICENTENNIAL COMMISSION OF FLORIDA,
SAMUEL PROCTOR, *General Editor.*

A FACSIMILE REPRODUCTION
OF THE 1823 EDITION
WITH PREFATORY MATERIAL, INTRODUCTION,
AND INDEX ADDED.

NEW MATERIAL COPYRIGHT © 1977
BY THE BOARD OF REGENTS
OF THE STATE OF FLORIDA.

Library of Congress Cataloging in Publication Data

Vignoles, Charles Blacker, 1793–1875.
    Observations upon the Floridas.

    (Bicentennial Floridiana facsimile series)
    Photoreprint ed. orignally published by E. Bliss and E. White,
New York.
    "A University of Florida book."
    1. Florida—History—To 1821. 2. Florida—Description and tra-
vel—To 1865. I. Title. II. Series.
F314.V53   1977   975.9   76–39956
ISBN 0–8130–0421–7

BICENTENNIAL COMMISSION OF FLORIDA.

―――――

Governor Reubin O'D. Askew, *Honorary Chairman*
Lieutenant Governor J. H. Williams, *Chairman*
Harold W. Stayman, Jr., *Vice Chairman*
William R. Adams, *Executive Director*

Dick J. Batchelor, Orlando
Johnnie Ruth Clarke, St. Petersburg
A. H. "Gus" Craig, St. Augustine
James J. Gardener, Fort Lauderdale
Jim Glisson, Tavares
Mattox Hair, Jacksonville
Thomas L. Hazouri, Jacksonville
Ney C. Landrum, Tallahassee
Mrs. Raymond Mason, Jacksonville
Carl C. Mertins, Jr., Pensacola
Charles E. Perry, Miami
W. E. Potter, Orlando
F. Blair Reeves, Gainesville

Richard R. Renick, Coral Gables
Jane W. Robinson, Cocoa
Mrs. Robert L. Shevin, Tallahassee
Don Shoemaker, Miami
Mary L. Singleton, Jacksonville
Bruce A. Smathers, Tallahassee
Alan Trask, Fort Meade
Edward J. Trombetta, Tallahassee
Ralph D. Turlington, Tallahassee
William S. Turnbull, Orlando
Robert Williams, Tallahassee
Lori Wilson, Merritt Island

GENERAL EDITOR'S
PREFACE.

═══════════

FLORIDA in its own special way has helped to shape the history of the world. The flags of Spain, England, and France have flown at one time or another over this land, whose recorded history was already more than 300 years old when, in 1821, it realized its final destiny and became part of the United States. Some of the world's most colorful personalities have moved across her stage. Conquistadors, missionaries, Indians, runaway slaves, pirates, roustabouts of every variety, land speculators, soldiers of fortune, and men and women of different religious and ethnic backgrounds, nationalities, and political persuasions have come to Florida and have made an impact on the area. There were a few scattered settlements along the Atlantic and Gulf coasts by the beginning of the nineteenth century, and there had been some exploration of the interior. Yet, except for North Florida, little was then known of this virtually trackless wilderness of forest and swamp land. In the 1760s and 1770s, before the American Revolution, the British had mapped the coastal areas, and travelers like Bartram had described the flora and fauna, the wildlife, Indian settlements, and the other strange and exotic things which they had observed as they meandered through the area.

By the time the territory became American, the maps had become outdated and the descriptive accounts were no longer pertinent. There was need for writers, cartographers, and geographers to reinvestigate and to describe this newly acquired territory. One of these writers was Charles Vignoles, whose *Observations upon the Floridas* is one of the volumes in the Bicentennial Floridiana Facsimile Series. It has been edited by John Hebron Moore of the Florida State University. The annexation of Florida, Vignoles wrote, has "advanced the soil of the Union to the very verge of the Tropics, and by placing the ports from the mouths of the Mississippi round to Amelia island, under the American flag, has hermetically closed all approaches to our interior." The area was now ready for American settlement.

Charles Vignoles was an Englishman by birth, a civil and topographical engineer, who had spent considerable time in America. He had lived and worked in Charleston, South Carolina, before moving to St. Augustine in August 1821, just one month after the American flag had been raised over this former Spanish colony. Vignoles was named surveyor and civil engineer for St. Augustine, and he became "Public Translator and Interpreter of French and Spanish languages" for East Florida. Vignoles was intrigued with all that he saw, and he decided to prepare a new map of Florida and to write a handbook for settlers.

The map was based upon Vignoles' survey of the coast from the St. Marys River south to Cape Florida. He talked to the few fishermen and farmers he found living in the area, and he checked the maps and charts which earlier cartographers—De Brahm, Romans, Gauld—had drawn. Georgia's Surveyor-General made available the documents compiled when the Georgia-Florida boundary line had been drawn. Vignoles' knowledge of the St. Marys River came from the manuscript survey made by Zephaniah Kingsley of Fort George Island. Pilots at Cape Florida supplied information, and the manuscripts and published works of many travelers were checked.

Vignoles' *Observations* provides a brief history of Florida from the time of its "discovery" in 1497 by John Cabot to the American annexation in 1821. It is mainly, however, about the practical things that would interest a settler contemplating a move to Florida. A man coming into an unknown area would want to know if he could sustain his family, if there was a way to secure needed supplies, and if the area was safe from Indian attack. He would be curious about the climate, soil conditions, and the availability of land. Based upon his own observations and the knowledge of others, Vignoles supplied this information. Vignoles was enamored of Florida; his work provides ample evidence of this.

"The rains and dews" were not at all troublesome, he wrote. They "create at most seasons such a luxuriant vegetation, that the surface of the earth is never without good verdure." Even after the most torrid days, he found the nights delightfully refreshing. Vignoles discovered that "a sheet of clean writing paper or a silk handkerchief placed in the hat keeps the head cool, when necessity requires an exposure to the summer sun." The climate was excellent "for patients of a consumptive habit." There was no danger from the night air, and he had seen "native and foreign ladies walking till late in the moonlight on summer and autumn evenings, with only the slight coverings on their head of their lace veils or *mantillas,* and many even without these."

Charles Vignoles was basically a publicist, and a successful one at that. Although his map was not perfect, as he admitted, and there are inaccuracies in his book, they were reliable documents. Sales for his products did not flourish, but *Observations upon the Floridas* did help to attract settlers to Florida, and it helped to orient these immigrants to a new land and to a new way of life.

The copy of Vignoles' book available for reproduction here by offset lithography unfortunately carries corrections, handwritten in ink by a former owner, of typographical errors and grammatical lapses. We hope the reader will not find these emendations distracting.

We also publish in this volume, as an item of historical interest, an article on Florida co-authored by Vignoles for the *Encyclopaedia Metropolitana,* published in London from 1817 to 1845. This is possibly the first article about Florida as a territory of the United States to be published in an encyclopedia. The printing here is not a facsimile. The copy has been newly set, and we have made no effort to reproduce the encyclopedia's format.

Observations upon the Floridas is one of the twenty-five rare and out-of-print Florida books that are being reprinted by the University Presses of Florida in co-operation with the American Revolution Bicentennial Commission of Florida. Each volume is being edited by an eminent scholar who has also written an incisive introduction and has compiled an index.

John Hebron Moore, editor of the Vignoles volume, is a native of Mississippi, and he holds his degrees from Mississippi State University, University of Mississippi, and Emory University. He was a member of the history faculty and chairman of the Department of History, University of Mississippi. Dr. Moore has also served as editor of the *Journal of Mississippi History.* He has been professor of history at the Florida State University, and is now chairman of the history department. He is the author of two books, several essays, and a number of articles which have appeared in scholarly journals. Professor Moore is a specialist on the economic and agricultural history of the South before the Civil War.

The Library of Congress provided a copy of the Vignoles map for reproduction here.

SAMUEL PROCTOR
General Editor of the
BICENTENNIAL FLORIDIANA
FACSIMILE SERIES

University of Florida

INTRODUCTION.

———

BECAUSE it was written soon after Spanish Florida was ceded to the United States, Charles Blacker Vignoles' *Observations upon the Floridas* (1823) is a valuable source of historical information on that new American territory. Furthermore, the author's subsequent career gives this work added interest as a historical document. Vignoles, who had been practicing his profession for only a few years when he prepared his commentary on Florida, subsequently became one of the great civil engineers of Victorian England, famous for railroads and bridges that he constructed in the British Isles, and on the continents of Europe and South America.[1]

From the moment of his birth on May 31, 1793, Vig-

noles led an extraordinarily interesting life. His fore-
bears for several generations had been professional
soldiers in the British Army, and his father, Charles
Henry Vignoles, held the rank of captain in the Forty-
third Foot Regiment (Monmouthshire Light Infantry)
when the boy was born. Captain Vignoles had previously been a secretary to Prince Edward, Duke of
Kent and father of Queen Victoria, and he continued to
enjoy the esteem of the royal family after rejoining his
regiment upon the outbreak of the war with Revolutionary France. In the autumn of 1793 Captain Vignoles sailed for the West Indies with the Forty-third
Light Infantry. Despite the obvious dangers of a military campaign in the tropics, the captain's young wife,
Camilla, and their infant son, Charles, accompanied
him in accordance with the custom of the British Army
in the late eighteenth century. Vignoles' regiment of
600 men was part of a task force numbering about
7,000, which was commanded by Lieutenant General
Sir Charles Grey. A squadron of nineteen warships
flying the flag of Admiral Sir John Jervis convoyed
Grey's troops and provided them with naval support
during the campaign. General Grey's mission was to
seize and occupy the French Windward Islands—Martinique, St. Lucia, and Guadeloupe—and then to re-
enforce with his surplus troops another British army
operating on St. Domingue.[2]

Elements of General Grey's command invaded Martinique on February 5, 1794, and after severe fighting
compelled General Donatien Rochambeau (of American
Revolutionary War fame) to surrender, on March 25, all
French forces on the island. Grey then attacked St. Lucia
on April 2, receiving the capitulation of the island's

French garrison two days later. Early in the morning of April 11, Admiral Jervis' warships landed General Grey's regiments on the southern shore of Pointe-à-Pitre Bay, near the port town of the same name. Before dawn, British regular soldiers and a detachment of sailors took Fort la Fleur d'Epée by assault. The French defenders then abandoned the town of Pointe-à-Pitre and Fort St. Louis to the invaders and withdrew all their forces from Grand Terre Island to Basse Terre, the larger and southernmost of Guadeloupe's two main islands. The British, after consolidating their hold on Grande Terre Island, launched April 14 an offensive against the French fortifications on Basse Terre. When resistance in the principal strong points at Palmiste and Houelmont quickly collapsed, General Collot on April 21 surrendered all his surviving soldiers. With this spectacular victory, General Grey had achieved his goals, and the British appeared to have attained supremacy in the West Indies, except for Cayenne and St. Domingue.

Within a few weeks after Collot's capitulation, however, disaster overwhelmed the victorious British forces most unexpectedly. During May, yellow fever swept with devastating effect through Admiral Jervis' ships and throughout the garrisons on the recently conquered islands. Then, at a moment when both the British land and sea forces were almost incapacitated by the terrible *vomito negro*, the French in force reinvaded Guadeloupe by sea, achieving a stunning surprise.

The fleet of three frigates and four transports which achieved this great feat of arms had sailed from Rochefort for Guadeloupe on April 23 with more than 1,500 regular soldiers on board. Victor Hugues, a civilian,

commanded the expedition as Commissioner of Guadeloupe and agent for the French National Convention.
Hugues had been born at Marseilles of a lower middle
class family. Lacking the advantage of an education, he
went to the French West Indies in his youth to seek his
fortune, working at a variety of jobs on Guadeloupe
and St. Domingue. At the beginning of the French Revolution, Hugues was employed with a brother and an
uncle in a bakery on St. Domingue supplying the army
with bread. During the civil struggles preceding the invasion of the island by the British, Hugues' brother and
uncle were killed, and he was deported to France; He
had apparently been associated with the Jacobin clubs
founded by Commissioner Léger Félicité Sonthonax,
who had freed the slaves on St. Domingue, for Hugues
immediately became intimate with the local Jacobins in
the port city of Rochefort. When a revolutionary tribunal was organized there in October 1793, to cope with
disloyalty in the navy as well as in the city, Hugues was
named public prosecutor. He displayed such zeal in that
office that he was asked to fill a similar position in the
more important port of Brest when a revolutionary
tribunal was established there in December. Hugues'
effectiveness in bringing royalists and anti-revolution-
ists to the guillotine attracted favorable notice from
Jacobin leaders in Paris, and he was chosen for the
difficult tasks of imposing the authority of the National
Convention on the rebellious planters of Guadeloupe,
and of implementing the decree of February 11 abolishing slavery in the French colonies.[3]

Good fortune sailed with Commissioner Hugues when
he departed from Rochefort. Although it was not known
in France at the time the fleet put out to sea that the

British had taken possession of Guadeloupe, Hugues' squadron made landfall off Pointe-à-Pitre without having made contact with the enemy navy anywhere on the voyage. By catastrophically bad judgment, Grey and Jervis had taken the entire British flotilla on a tour of inspection to St. Kitts, leaving the army wide open to attack from the sea. As a result, the French vessels were able to enter the bay of Pointe-à-Pitre on June 6 without opposition. Learning only then that the British were in control of all Guadeloupe, Hugues landed his troops on the opposite side of the island at the port of Le Moule. From there he led his force across the island to attack Fort la Fleur d'Epée, which was situated on a height that overlooked the town of Pointe-à-Pitre and Fort St. Louis, from the rear. The French regulars after making several costly assaults eventually swarmed over the walls and killed or captured most of the garrison. Lieutenant-Colonel Drummond, commander of the Forty-third Foot, cut his way out of the fort with about forty men and escaped across the channel to Basse Terre.

During the next three weeks the victorious and still healthy French regulars established themselves firmly in the forts, la Fleur d'Epée and St. Louis, and in the town of Pointe-à-Pitre, easily repelling feeble British attacks carried out in desperation on July 1. After this decisive defeat, General Grey withdrew his disease-riddled regiments to defensive positions on Basse Terre, where yellow fever daily reduced their numbers. General Grey as commander-in-chief of British forces in the Windward Islands then transferred his headquarters to Martinique, leaving Brigadier General Graham in command of the troops left on Basse Terre.

Soon after landing on Guadeloupe, the unseasoned soldiers from metropolitan France began, like the British, to succumb to the raging yellow fever epidemic. The resourceful Jacobin proconsul, however, contrived to re-enforce his regular troops with mulattoes and blacks who were immune to the fever. To this end, he published the decree of the National Convention abolishing slavery, and he summoned all loyal Frenchmen to fight against the British invaders. When many hundreds of grateful ex-slaves responded to Hugues' call to the colors, he provided them with arms and uniforms and organized them into regiments. After he had given his black recruits a smattering of training, the commissioner began a campaign on September 26 to recapture Basse Terre. The French made rapid progress after establishing a base of operations on Basse Terre, for General Graham had concentrated most of his army of sick and dying men in a large fortified camp called Berville. On October 6, after beating off five waves of attackers—mostly black soldiers—Graham surrendered all of his army except for a 600-man contingent holding Fort Matilda under command of elderly Major General Prescott. These troops were besieged until December 10 when they were evacuated by the British fleet.

Commissioner Hugues instituted a reign of terror on Guadeloupe as soon as he had gained control of Pointe-à-Pitre. Intending to wipe out the planter class, who had generally sided with the British, he executed dozens of royalists with the guillotine and sent many hundreds more before firing squads. Horrified by the treatment that Maximilien Robespierre's disciple was meting out to his own countrymen, the British accepted without question reports that Hugues had ordered captured

British soldiers and their wives and children to be bayoneted to death. Such an atrocity did occur, but the likelihood is that undisciplined black troops killed these people in the excitement of storming a fort.

Whether or not Hugues was really the bloodthirsty monster whom British propaganda described, he undeniably was a politician-soldier of genius. In the face of overwhelming British seapower, Hugues succeeded in driving the British army out of St. Lucia and several small islands as well as Guadeloupe, and he raised rebellions among the black and Indian populations of British St. Vincent and Jamaica. Although the British were eventually able to repossess themselves of most of the Windward Islands, crushing the slave revolts, they were unable because of Hugues' work to shake the hold of the French on Guadeloupe until Napoleon tried to restore slavery there in 1802.

The experience of the Vignoles family throws a different light on Commissioner Victor Hugues from the one by which he is usually viewed by English-speaking historians. Captain Vignoles' regiment served with distinction during the victorious campaigns on Martinique, St. Lucia, and Guadeloupe as part of a brigade commanded by Prince Edward, who held the rank of major general at that time. As a result of heavy losses from battle and yellow fever, the Forty-third's ten companies were reduced to a handful of invalids by October 6, 1794, when Graham's command laid down their arms. Captain Vignoles had been one of the first of the officers to become a battle casualty. He was severely wounded on June 6 when Hugues' regulars stormed Fort la Fleur d'Epée with the bayonet, and he was taken prisoner along with the surviving British soldiers and civilians who had taken refuge in the fort. His wife and baby also fell with him into the hands of the enemy, along with the other British civilians.

Instead of being massacred, as Hugues' reputation would lead one to expect, the wounded British captain and his wife and baby were placed in charge of a local French merchant named Courtois. When all three members of the English family contracted yellow fever, Courtois' wife and servants cared for their charges until Captain Vignoles and his wife both died of the terrible disease. Madame Courtois provided a black wet nurse for the infant when his mother became ill, and nursed the child through an extended sickness until he recovered his health completely. Monsieur Courtois then wrote with Commissioner Hugues' consent to Dr. Charles Hutton, the baby's maternal grandfather, informing him of the plight of young Vignoles and suggesting that someone be sent to claim him for his family.

Upon receiving this news, Dr. Hutton persuaded his only son, George Henry Hutton, a captain in the Royal Artillery, to undertake the mission.[4] Captain Hutton then took passage to Martinique where he applied to General Grey for permission to proceed to General Graham's headquarters at Camp Berville on Guadeloupe. Obtaining the necessary credentials, Hutton soon afterward went ashore at the British position on Basse Terre, where he found that his services as an artillery expert were urgently required because yellow fever had felled all of the force's artillery officers. Temporarily abandoning his mission of mercy, Captain Hutton took command of General Graham's guns, and directed the work of the British batteries in the heavy fighting that preceded the capitulation of the army. Just before the surrender, he received a face wound that cost him an eye. When Hutton had sufficiently recovered from his injury to permit him to travel, Commissioner Hugues himself paroled the English artilleryman so that he could carry the Vignoles baby to England, and provided them with transportation to the nearest British island. Because of this uncharacteristic act of chivalry, Dr. Hutton's family saw Hugues from a viewpoint quite different from that of the general British public.

When Prince Edward, the Duke of Kent, learned that Captain Vignoles' child had survived the deaths of his parents and had reached England safely, he took action on the child's behalf. Wishing to provide for the orphaned child of his former secretary, who had lost his life serving in a unit commanded by himself, the duke arranged for the appointment of the infant, Charles B. Vignoles, as an ensign in his father's regiment, with a commission dated October 25, 1794. This sinecure authorized the child to draw an ensign's half-pay of about thirty pounds sterling a year until he became old enough to join the regiment. In this fashion, his royal patron ensured that young Vignoles would not become a financial burden to Dr. Hutton, his guardian and his grandfather. Unfortunately, this royal patronage also made Charles Blacker financially independent, a situation that encouraged him as a teen-ager to rebel against his grandfather's authority to a degree which cost him eventually an inheritance. Captain Vignoles, himself, had left nothing to his son except a claim to a land grant in East Florida.

Until he was eighteen years old, Charles Vignoles lived with his grandfather and Dr. Hutton's unmarried daughter, Isabella, who was very kind to the child. Dr. Charles Hutton, professor of mathematics at the Royal Military Academy at Woolwich from 1773 to 1807, was a very unusual man.[5] Born in 1737 at Newcastle-on-Tyne, the youngest son of a coal miner, he worked for a while as a "hewer" in the mine where his stepfather was a foreman. When young Hutton showed an exceptional aptitude for books, his stepfather took him out of the pits and sent him to a local school. Charles began teaching when he was eighteen, and later, in 1760, he opened his own school of mathematics in Newcastle. He also tutored the children of a family of the local gentry who owned an extensive library, and thus, he had access to advanced mathematical studies. During the 1760s he attained considerable local fame as a teacher and published a textbook on the teaching of mathematics which he had prepared for use in his own school.

By winning a competitive examination held in 1773, Hutton obtained a prestigious post as professor of mathematics at the Royal Military Academy. This institution, located outside London near the Woolwich arsenal, provided technical training for artillery and engineering officers. It was also for many decades the only school of engineering in the British Isles. As a measure of the professional and social status associated with this office, Professor Hutton was elected in 1774 a fellow of the Royal Society. During the next quarter century, he earned a reputation as one of England's leading mathematicians. As a result of reports published for him by the Royal Society on the mathematics of ballistics, on the force generated by exploding gunpowder, and on measuring the density of the earth, Professor Hutton was awarded the LL.D. degree in 1779 by the University of Edinburgh. While a member of the faculty at Woolwich, he published nine books on mathematics, including a text used in the college for many years, and a study of the mathematics of arches as related to bridge building. He also published tables of logarithms and a work on conic sections. As a mathematician who specialized in the practical application of mathematics to engineering problems, Dr. Hutton became a consultant of several of the leading English civil engineers of late eighteenth and early nineteenth centuries. He also became personally acquainted with George III's sons, Princes Frederick and Edward, who were keenly interested in the military college at Woolwich. This was social success, indeed, for a man who had risen from the laboring class to the top of his profession.

While gaining national professional recognition as a mathematician, Dr. Hutton also made a considerable fortune as a real-estate developer. Intending to build a house for himself on Shooter's Hill, he acquired some land bordering on the Woolwich Common. Shortly afterward, the Royal Military Academy was moved away from the grounds of the Woolwich arsenal and established at a new site fronting on the common. This move greatly increased the value of Hutton's property, and he quickly capitalized on his advantage by opening a residential development. The houses he built sold so well that he soon became wealthy. He subsequently purchased a London townhouse on Bedford Row, and made many successful investments in a number of engineering projects. With the fees earned as a consultant and the income from his business investments, Hutton lived more like a member of the gentry than the usual professor.

Professor Hutton probably took personal charge of his grandson's education; there is no surviving evidence to suggest that Vignoles ever attended a public school. It is certain, however, that besides mastering mathematics, he became fluent in French, Spanish, and German, and also learned to speak a little Dutch. From his grandfather and possibly from other professors at Woolwich, Vignoles gained a considerable knowledge of the techniques of civil and military engineering. Inasmuch as technical training was provided for British army officers during that era only in artillery and engineering, young Vignoles could hardly have been better placed to learn the basics of his future profession.

Vignoles was not an enthusiastic student and displayed little interest in the study of mathematics. As a result, his grandfather decided against an engineering career for him. Soon after the family moved to London in 1807, following Dr. Hutton's retirement, plans were made to train the boy in the law. Dr. Hutton paid a prominent firm of solicitors, which had offices on Doctor's Common, to accept Vignoles as an apprentice. But these were exciting war years, and Vignoles was too adventurous a lad to become absorbed in studying law at a moment when England was locked in her struggle with Napoleon. Sometime in 1812 Vignoles abandoned his studies in flagrant disregard of his grandfather's wishes and went to Portugal to offer his services to the army commanded by the Duke of Wellington. Although Vignoles did not succeed in obtaining an official position with the British expeditionary forces, he did see something of the conflict on the Peninsula and was present at the Battle of Vittorio on June 21, 1813. Deciding to become an army officer like his father, Vignoles knew that he needed some training in military matters before taking up his commission in the Forty-third Regiment.

Furious at Vignoles' flouting of his authority and his disinclination for serious work, Dr. Hutton disinherited his grandson for leaving the law firm, and never again permitted the boy to enter the house on Bedford Row during the remainder of his lifetime. He did relent to a degree in 1813, and arranged for a friend and former colleague, Thomas Leybourne, professor of mathematics at the Royal Military College, to take Vignoles into his home as a student and house guest. Although never a member of the corps of cadets at Sandhurst, Vignoles apparently attended that institution in an informal capacity for about three months in the autumn of 1813. Toward the close of what must have been a very abbreviated course in military science, Vignoles was introduced by Professor Leybourne to his patron, the Duke of Kent, who volunteered to write on the boy's behalf, both to the Duke of Wellington and to the commander of the Forty-third Regiment. As a direct result of the duke's personal interest in his career, Vignoles was posted soon after receiving his commission in November 1813, to the Fourteenth Light Dragoons (Duchess of York's Own, popularly called the York Chasseurs), a cavalry regiment serving under Wellington. As an untrained officer and an unskilled horseman, however, Vignoles was not sent to join the Chasseurs in Spain, but was ordered to report to the regiment's depot on the Isle of Wight. As an ensign on active duty, Vignoles was paid only 100 pounds sterling a year (approximately $500), out of which he was required to furnish his own uniforms and equipment. With some dismay, he wrote to his fiancée that "I must begin for the first time in my life to be economical."

Quickly becoming dissatisfied with the routine duties to which he was assigned, Vignoles petitioned the Duke of Kent for assistance in obtaining a transfer to an infantry regiment that was then preparing for active service. Field Marshal Frederick Augustus, Duke of York and commander-in-chief of the forces in Great Britain and Ireland, quickly approved Vignoles' request for reassignment to the Fourth Battalion of the First Foot (the Royal Scots), the Duke of Kent's own regiment. In January 1814 Ensign Vignoles reported for duty at the First Regiment's headquarters in the field, then located in the Dutch town of Williamstadt. Soon after Vignoles arrived in Holland, qualified army officers were invited to apply for a vacancy in the separate Corps of Engineers. Passing an easy examination, Vignoles was appointed assistant-engineer, but Colonel Müller, the commanding officer of the First Foot, refused to release him because the Royal Scots were about to take part in an assault upon the French fortress of Bergen op Zoom.

The preceding November some of the Dutch had revolted against the French at a time when armies of the Allies were moving against France on several fronts. During December 1813, a small British army under command of Sir Thomas Graham landed in Holland with orders to support the revolt and to drive out the

French. The beleaguered French withdrew to a fortified line running from Antwerp to Flushing, but not before defeating the pursuing British in a battle before Antwerp. Checked at that point, General Graham decided to try to break through the enemy line by capturing Bergen op Zoom, a seventeenth-century fortified town.[6]

Hoping to surprise the French garrison, Graham launched a night attack against Bergen op Zoom on March 8, 1814, employing four separate columns of about 1,000 men each. As in most complicated night maneuvers, Graham's battle plan immediately led to confusion. One of his columns crossed the shallow Zoom River an hour early, achieving the surprise in one sector that Graham had been counting on everywhere, but this success was gained at the expense of the other three columns which crossed the river later. Meeting little resistance, the infantrymen of the first column broke through lightly manned defenses into the town. When the other three columns splashed across the ice-filled Zoom, however, they encountered an aroused enemy who fiercely resisted. Nevertheless, two of these columns were able to force their way into the fortress. A fourth column came under such heavy fire while approaching the fortress that some of its units were driven back in disorder. After the disrupted battalions were reformed, they were led around the fortress to make an attack from the rear. Finding a gate on that side practically unguarded, the troops of the fourth column also entered the city. By 1:00 A.M., ten of the sixteen bastions of the fortress were in English hands.

General Graham, believing that victory was virtually

achieved, left the city to bring up reserves which he
intended to use to consolidate the British positions in
the town. But, soon after his departure, the situation
drastically changed. The French, who had been concentrating in the center of the town, launched a series of
well organized counterattacks which overwhelmed, one
by one, the British units scattered around the periphery
of the fortress. Only the English Foot Guards were
able to withstand for a time the fury of the French
onslaught. Defending their position in the Orange Bas-
tion with grim determination, the Guards repeatedly
exchanged attacks and counterattacks with the French
until heavy losses of men finally compelled the English
to capitulate. When General Graham finally reached
Bergen with his reserve regiments the next morning,
he found the French already in complete control of the
battlefield. Not less than 2,500 British officers and soldiers had been killed, wounded, or captured in this unhappy conclusion to a generally disastrous campaign.

The Royal Scots, under Colonel Müller's uninspired
leadership, had done nothing to distinguish themselves.
As the rearmost regiment in the column commanded by
General Carleton on the right, the Scots had forded the
river under light cannon fire and were stationed outside the Water Gate as a reserve, while the troops in
the van pushed through the gate into the town. Once
inside the walls, Carleton's troops became scattered
in the darkness, losing all semblance of organization.
When the French, attacking in column, struck these
dispersed units, General Carleton himself was killed
almost immediately. In the confused street fighting that

ensued, no one thought to bring up the 600 men of the Scottish First Regiment from the Water Gate. Being unwilling to act without direct orders, Colonel Müller held the Scots in position outside the citadel for six critical hours while the remainder of Carleton's troops were being slaughtered in the streets and in the bastions along the wall. As soon as they had crushed the English units in the town, the French occupied the bastions in the vicinity of the Water Gate and directed a heavy fire upon the Royals standing in the open. Around 7:00 A.M. Müller became convinced that his troops could neither hold their exposed position nor retreat across the river without being annihilated, and he decided to surrender his regiment without having struck a blow at the enemy.

Armed with his sword and a pike taken from a wounded sergeant, Ensign Vignoles had struggled across the Zoom River and its bordering marshes with a company of the Royal Scots, only to stand for many hours, muddy, wet, and freezing, outside the fortress. When Colonel Müller eventually decided to lay down his arms, he selected Vignoles to act as his emissary to the enemy commander because the young officer spoke French. Vignoles entered the town under a flag of truce and obtained an audience with General Bizanet. Anxious to terminate the fighting before British reenforcements arrived, Bizanet promptly agreed to accept Müller's proffered capitulation of his regiment. In accordance with the French general's instructions, Vignoles waved a white flag from the ramparts as a signal for the Royals to lay down their arms and march into the town as prisoners of war. By 9:00 A.M., March 9, the last of the British troops taking part in the assault on Bergen had complied with the terms of surrender.

The French garrison, which numbered less than 3,000 men, treated the British prisoners with unusual humanity. They provided them with food and shelter, and permitted them to move freely about the streets. The following day, a convention was signed between the French and British high commands freeing all of the prisoners on condition they not engage in further hostilities against France during the war. Vignoles, having performed creditably as a military diplomat on this unhappy occasion, found himself in high favor with Colonel Müller and with the rest of the army establishment in Holland.

Because of the terms of capitulation which ended the battle of Bergen op Zoom, the Royal Scots returned to England before Napoleon abdicated his throne in April 1814. At Hilsea Barracks in Portsmouth, the Royals were refitted for further active service because the Scottish First Regiment had been assigned to a force of about 15,000 men that was to be transported to Canada to take part in an invasion of the northern United States.

The Royal Scots sailed in several warships because there was a shortage of troop transports. In May 1814 Ensign Vignoles and two companies of the Fourth Battalion boarded H.M.S. *Leopard*, a frigate that had become infamous to Americans in 1807 when it attacked the United States frigate *Chesapeake*. The other two companies were loaded on the *Diomede*. After an uneventful crossing, during which the officers entertained themselves by presenting theatrical productions, the *Leopard* came ingloriously to grief at the mouth of the St. Lawrence River. Running upon one of those "unchartered rocks" which had claimed so many British naval vessels in war and peace, the frigate went down June 28 near the island of Anticosti. The crew and military passengers reached shore safely, although suffering from exposure to the severe weather conditions. Vignoles was in the first contingent of survivors of the shipwreck to reach Quebec, and his trip upriver had taken seventeen days.

As a result of this experience, Vignoles contracted a case of pneumonia which incapacitated him for several weeks. So many of the enlisted men of the two shipwrecked companies also became seriously ill that the whole Fourth Battalion was regarded as unfit for combat. Yet, the shipwreck had an unexpectedly happy outcome for the army officers and men; while they were recuperating at Quebec, the First Battalion saw action against the Americans on the Niagara River front where those experienced soldiers learned a grudging respect for their opponents. In hand-to-hand fighting at Lundy's Lane, the battalion lost 172 men out of a total strength of 200.[7]

As Vignoles apparently had experienced enough fighting at Bergen op Zoom to satsfy his thirst for military glory, he was able to endure philosophically the Fourth Battalion's extended period of inactivity at Quebec. He passed his leisure time pleasantly by acting in plays put on by the junior officers and by cultivating the friendship of Colonel Müller. Meanwhile, the Forty-third Regiment, in which Vignoles was originally commissioned, and a squadron of the Fourteenth Cavalry Regiment to which he had been briefly attached, took part in the disastrous battle of New Orleans.

At the close of hostilities in America, fortune again favored Vignoles and the Fourth Battalion. When the Royals embarked for England, Vignoles, recently promoted to the rank of lieutenant, and the battalion were among the last of the regiment to leave Canada. While the regiment was in transit, Napoleon returned from Elba, and the war with France began again. As a result, the first units of the Royal Scots to reach port in England were rushed immediately to the Lowlands to reenforce Wellington's hard-pressed army. By dint of hard marching, the Third Battalion arrived in time to be mauled severely at Quatre Bras by General François Kellermann's cavalry.[8] Vignoles and the Fourth, however, did not reach Spithead until July 15, when the final campaign against Napoleon was already over. Thus, Vignoles, through no fault of his own, emerged unscathed from three wars in which many others had become casualties.

With the conclusion of the conflict on the continent, the First Regiment settled down at its regular station at Edinburgh. After a short period of service there, Vignoles assumed command of a small detachment manning Fort Williams, a small outpost in northern Scotland. There he remained for several months, dreading the inevitable day when he would be put on half-pay. Because he had less seniority than most of the lieutenants in his regiment, Vignoles had virtually no chance of remaining permanently with the regiment while a general postwar demobilization of Britain's military machine was in process. As he had often done before, Vignoles sought assistance at this juncture from the Duke of Kent. His Royal Highness could do nothing on Vignoles' behalf this time, however, for he was being overwhelmed by similar requests from hundreds of unemployed officers.

In March 1816 Vignoles was placed on the inactive list. Unwilling to pursue another profession, he resorted to extraordinary means to stay in the military. At his own expense he journeyed to the French city of Valenciennes, where the headquarters of Wellington's Second Division was located. There he offered his services as an unpaid volunteer aide-de-camp to the commanding general, Sir Thomas Brisbane, whom he had known in Canada. Major General Brisbane, who had a heavy burden of paperwork to carry, gladly accepted Vignoles' service. In hope of finding a permanent post in the standing army through Brisbane's influence, Vignoles assisted the general until funds and credit were almost exhausted. He reluctantly returned to England in April 1817.

In London, Vignoles attempted to make a reconciliation with his grandfather, but Dr. Hutton sternly rejected all his overtures. Realizing that he must rely entirely on his own resources for the present, Vignoles sought employment, only to find that the city was swarming with a host of demobilized army and navy officers in similar circumstances. With his financial situation becoming desperate, Vignoles learned from Professor Leybourne that Sir Gregor MacGregor, a former officer in the Forty-second Regiment (the Royal Highlanders, or the "Black Watch") who had become a general in the South American independence movement led by

Simon Bolívar, was recruiting personnel for the rebel army.[9] Making further inquiries, Vignoles was informed that Whitehall secretly was supporting the independence movement and that high government officials approved MacGregor's enlistment of unemployed officers. Making contact without difficulty with Venezuelan agents in London, Vignoles applied for a position as an engineer in their military establishment. His application was promptly accepted, and he sailed for the Caribbean August 3, 1817, in company with several other English half-pay army and navy officers.

Arriving at the Danish island of St. Thomas September 27, 1817, Vignoles learned that MacGregor had left Caracas, hoping to raise money and men for his cause in the United States. Knowing that America had long been anxious to acquire Spanish Florida, Vignoles learned from the United States consul that merchants in New Orleans had advanced more than $150,000 to MacGregor to supply a rebel army that he was assembling at Fernandina on Amelia Island off northeast Florida. Because his government wished Spain to be expelled from Florida by any means, the American consul arranged to transport Vignoles and his companions to Fernandina on an American schooner.

Arriving at Fernandina, Vignoles quickly became disenchanted with the independence movement. MacGregor's band of followers appeared more like a congregation of outlaws than a patriot army, and British officers in the rebel service decried the leadership of Bolívar and the long-range prospects of the movement. As a result, Vignoles decided not to join MacGregor. Instead, he took ship to Charleston, South Carolina, apparently with the intention of obtaining passage on a vessel bound for England.

In Charleston, Vignoles met friends of Dr. Hutton who suggested that he establish himself there as a civil engineer, which were in short supply in the city. He could not afford to go into business for himself immediately, so Vignoles applied to the state engineer of South Carolina, and was hired as assistant civil engineer, surveyor, and draftsman at an annual salary of $1,000. This was regarded as a part-time job, and Vignoles was permitted to accept private contracts as a civil engineer. He opened an office in Charleston with J. Pettival as an associate.[10]

After having eked out an uncertain existence on a lieutenant's half-pay for two years, Vignoles found life pleasant in South Carolina. With money coming in from his state salary and from private surveys that he and Pettival were undertaking for local landowners, Vignoles enjoyed a welcome relief from financial pressure. Convinced by South Carolina's postwar prosperity that limitless opportunities existed for competent civil engineers, Vignoles was optimistic about his business prospects. He sent for his young wife, Mary, whom he had secretly married before leaving England, and their year-old daughter, Camilla. When they arrived in September 1818, Vignoles settled them in quarters at Fort Moultrie on Sullivans Island which the state provided to him without charge. A year later, a son was born, whom the couple christened Thomas in honor of Professor Leybourne.

Vignoles worked three years for South Carolina, helping prepare an official map of the state. During most of this period he was engaged in surveying the state's coast-line and drawing portions of the great map. Judged by his increases in salary, he must have pleased his superiors with his work. At the end of Vignoles' first year in the engineer's office, his annual salary was raised to $2,000. By 1820 he considered himself sufficiently well established as an engineer to relinquish his fixed salary, taking instead a contract to survey the southeastern boundaries of the state for a fee of $3,700. During his last two years in South Carolina, his private business had increased even more rapidly than his work for the state. With the onset of the depression of 1819, however, Vignoles began to experience difficulty in collecting his fees for work done for the lowland planters.

When the map of South Carolina was ready for publication in 1820, Vignoles lost his lucrative connection with the state, and became wholly dependent on his private business.[11] As the depression deepened in the Charleston area, he began to think of moving to Florida. In preparation for the move, he broke up housekeeping in Charleston and carried his wife and children back to England.

Returning alone to Charleston, Vignoles was surprised to find that there was a need again for his services as a civil engineer. Because of the depression, many more pieces of real estate were changing hands than was normally the case, and each of them had to be surveyed. He was able to obtain all the work he and his partner could handle, but they continued to be plagued by the inability of their clients to pay their bills. He therefore considered himself fortunate to obtain a contract to map the city of Charleston for $500. Finishing this contract, he decided to investigate the business possibilities in St. Augustine, Florida.

Although he did not abandon his business contacts in Charleston, Vignoles moved his office to St. Augustine in August 1821, shortly after the territory became American. He quickly obtained a contract to prepare a map of the town similar to the one he had recently drawn for Charleston. Soon afterward, he was appointed surveyor and civil engineer for St. Augustine. His familiarity with several languages proved useful in this multi-lingual community, and in February 1822, William G. D. Worthington, territorial secretary and acting governor of East Florida, listed him as Public Translator and Interpretor of French and Spanish Languages in the "Register of Public Officials of East Florida."[12]

Despite his initially favorable reception in St. Augustine, Vignoles soon had reason to wonder whether his decision to move there from Charleston was well advised. American settlers were not flocking into Florida as he had expected, and an epidemic of yellow fever brought business almost to a standstill during the first half of 1822. Vignoles also encountered in Florida a prejudice against Englishmen that had been absent in South Carolina. Observing that this anti-British sentiment was costing him business, Vignoles began to consider whether he should take out United States citizenship. Yet he continued to believe that the stagnant economy of East Florida was a passing phase, and that Americans eventually would migrate into the new territory in large numbers.

In order to occupy his time profitably in a period when his services were not in demand, and also to lay

the foundation for a later business as a land agent,
Vignoles decided to prepare a new map of Florida
which he would publish in conjunction with a handbook
for immigrants. Once he had decided on this project, he
went to work with characteristic energy and enthusiasm. By December 1821 Vignoles had surveyed the
northeastern coast of Florida from the border of Georgia southward to the 27.5 degree of latitude, and had
drawn a map of that coastline. He presented a copy of
his map together with a description of the soil and geo-
graphic features of the area to Captain John R. Bell of
the United States War Department, apparently hoping
that he would be employed by the federal government
to map the whole littoral of Florida.[13] If so, he was
disappointed, but he was employed as a surveyor for
General Winfield Scott, who made a tour of inspection
during February 1822. Vignoles' duties took him to
Cape Florida, Cape Sable, the Tortugas, and up the
west coast to Tampa Bay.

Hardships that Vignoles encountered while making
the surveys for General Scott, including an episode in
which he was nearly drowned while swimming his horse
across a river, brought on a lengthy bout with "bilious
fever," which delayed for several weeks the completion
of the map and a volume of observations about Florida.
While recuperating from his illness, he traveled to several of the cities of the eastern seaboard, no doubt looking for business opportunities. If that was the case, he
failed to locate an attractive opening for his talents, for
he returned to St. Augustine and spent the summer
preparing the map and commentary for publication. In
September 1822 he carried his map and manuscript to

New York, where he arranged for the printing firm of Bliss and White to publish the book. Henry S. Tanner, of Philadelphia, prepared the engraving of the map.[14] Vignoles had decided, unwisely it turned out, to hold the copyright and to handle the distribution of the map and book himself rather than to surrender any of the proceeds from the sales to a publisher. In June he therefore placed a lengthy advertisement in several newspapers describing the map and book and announcing that both items would cost subscribers a total sum of no more than three dollars.[15] With the country deep in depression and with interest in Florida real estate at its lowest point in American history, Vignoles' venture failed miserably. The few copies of the set that he managed to sell did not cover the cost of publication, much less his living expenses in New York.[16]

Completely discouraged by the adverse effects that the depression had exerted on his business as a civil engineer, as well as by the unhappy outcome of his venture into publishing, Vignoles decided to return to England when he received news of Dr. Hutton's death. He was in severe financial difficulty when he left the United States, and although he had no reason to believe that his grandfather had reinstated him in the will, he hoped that his aunt, Isabella, might share her inheritance with him. Upon reaching London in late May 1823, Vignoles hastened to call upon his aunt, who welcomed him with affection. Although she was sympathetic about Vignoles' pecuniary distress, he learned that she was in no position to offer assistance to him.

Around 1815 Dr. Hutton had invested heavily in a company organized to construct a bridge across the

Thames River in London between Blackfriars Bridge and the old London Bridge. The elder John Rennie (1761-1821), famous for his canals and harbor works and a close friend of Dr. Hutton, was then erecting the highly successful Waterloo Bridge (it was opened in 1817), and he also designed and supervised the construction of the Southwark Bridge. Although Rennie had used granite in the Waterloo Bridge, he employed three 240-foot castiron arches resting on cypress pilings in the Southwark Bridge. Completed in 1819, Rennie's handsome castiron structure was widely acclaimed as a technological triumph, and the bridge inspired the subsequent widespread use of this new building material. The cost of construction, however, had enormously exceeded Rennie's estimates, and the stockholders in the Southwark company lost most of their investments. Dr. Hutton's fortune was almost wiped out in the debacle. Consequently, Vignoles' unmarried aunt inherited little from her father in 1823 other than his house on Bedford Row.

Although badly disappointed that his aunt could not help him establish a civil engineering office in England, Vignoles was soon to receive important benefits from the close association between Dr. Hutton and the Rennie family. Rennie's older son, Sir John Rennie, took over his father's business and continued it with great distinction, and in the process earned for himself a great reputation. Knowing that his father had felt responsible for bringing financial ruin to his friend, young Rennie considered himself obligated to assist Dr. Hutton's grandson. He therefore introduced Vignoles to members of his profession who could give him employment. Later, after Vignoles had demonstrated that he was an exceptionally competent and responsible engineer in his own right, Rennie helped him obtain contracts on an increasingly important scale. During this period a warm personal relationship developed between the two men, which ultimately brought a golden opportunity to Vignoles. This was an assignment as resident engineer for the Liverpool and Manchester Railroad Company during a crucial period in the construction of the famous line which inaugurated the steam railway era.

In 1825, with the success of his Stockton and Darlington coal-carrying railway assured, George Stephenson, the great advocate of steam locomotives, turned his attention to a far more ambitious project, the construction of a railroad connecting the booming manufacturing city of Manchester with the port of Liverpool. Stephenson was able to attract financial support for this scheme without difficulty because the growth of commerce between these two cities had outstripped the carrying capacity of the canals which had been the principal means of transportation in the first quarter of the nineteenth century. When Stephenson's company applied to Parliament for a charter, however, they encountered powerful opposition from agents of the Duke of Bridgewater, who controlled the canals, and from landowners who objected to the railway crossing their lands. Self-educated and inarticulate, Stephenson was an ineffective witness for the project before parliamentary committees in the spring of 1825, and his opponents trapped him into admission of errors in his surveys that led to the rejection of the application for a charter.[17]

A reorganized board of directors then turned to the younger John Rennie for assistance in obtaining the necessary charter for the projected railway. Indignant at being asked to share the building of the railway with another engineer, Stephenson withdrew from the company. Rennie accepted the appointment as chief engineer, but being occupied with other projects, he turned the task over to George, his younger brother, and to Charles Vignoles. George Rennie and Vignoles shrewdly reduced political opposition to the L & M by making minor changes in the route so as to avoid lands of persons who were adamantly opposed to the line. Vignoles also was successful in arranging an accommodation with the Duke of Bridgewater, which removed a major obstacle to incorporation of the company. During April 1826 Vignoles defended the company's request for a new act of incorporation before committees of the House of Lords and the House of Commons. In order to avoid some of the criticisms that had been directed at Stephenson's proposal to use locomotives rather than stationary steam engines as the motive power for the L & M railroad, Vignoles did not recommend either system in the plan he presented to Parliament. Vignoles' skillfully prepared surveys of the route won the endorsements of many prominent engineers consulted by the committee members, and he was credited by many contemporary observers with gaining approval of the act by his lucid and candid testimony. In any event, the charter of the L & M company was approved in late April 1826.

Having successfully made use of the Rennies to obtain the all-essential charter, the directors of the Liverpool and Manchester Railroad Company then decided to re-employ George Stephenson to take charge of the actual construction of the railroad. Although they knew that the Rennie firm had a greater reputation as civil engineers than did Stephenson, the Rennies' reputation had been acquired in the construction of harbors, canals, and bridges, while Stephenson was known to be the most successful builder of coal-mine railways in England. Although John Rennie was given the option of sharing the post of chief engineer with Stephenson, he knew that the former coal miner would not gracefully divide authority with anyone. He therefore withdrew from any further connection with the project.

Vignoles, who had been serving as the principal resident engineer of the railway since August 1825, was left in an unenviable position by John Rennie's departure. Although he held no official position with the Rennie firm, he had been appointed by John Rennie to his post with the L & M railroad. Stephenson, who was bitter toward the Rennies, naturally preferred his own assistants, and he particularly objected to being compelled by the directors to retain one of his rival's friends in a key position. Vignoles, however, had supporters of his own on the board, and their influence overrode for a time Stephenson's animosity toward him. From the beginning, however, it was clear to all concerned that Stephenson was determined to rid himself of Vignoles as soon as possible. Hence, Vignoles' work as an engineer, which had been regarded as exceptionally good while Rennie was chief engineer, was subjected to a steady fire of criticism by his new superior. Finally,

Stephenson was able to present evidence to the directors that Vignoles had made an error in his calculations while laying out a tunnel on the approach to Liverpool. Although Vignoles protested that the error was of minor consequence and easily corrected, Stephenson succeeded in having him removed from his post by a reluctant board. As a result of this clearly political dismissal, Vignoles left the L & M construction job with his reputation as an outstanding civil engineer undamaged. Thus, from his experience with the L & M, Vignoles gained invaluable publicity as a skilled railroad builder which subsequently brought him many offers from other railroad companies. He also was elected to the Institute of Civil Engineers in 1827.[18]

Although the Rennies, along with many other engineers of the time, still were not convinced while the L & M was under construction that steam locomotives were practical and economical sources of motive power, Vignoles agreed with Stephenson that these machines should be employed on the L & M railroad. In fact, he was so convinced that the future of overland transportation depended upon steam locomotives that he invested some of his hard-earned savings in John Ericsson's "Novelty," which competed unsuccessfully with Stephenson's "Rocket" in the famous trials held in October 1829 to determine which machine would be adopted by the L & M.

The reputation that he had acquired as resident engineer for the Liverpool and Manchester railroad brought a flood of business opportunities to Vignoles when he left the employ of the railway company. However, during the next three years he was engaged on several important civil engineering assignments of a traditional nature that had nothing to do with railroads, including a survey of the Isle of Man on behalf of the British government, improvements on the Oxford canal constructed originally by Thomas Telford, and a project to improve navigation on the Slaney River in Ireland, financed by the Earl of Portsmouth. With the railroad building mania gathering strength during the early 1830s, however, Vignoles was drawn back into railway construction. In 1830 he was appointed chief engineer of two different companies in Lancashire which were planning to build short coal-carrying lines. Under his supervision both steam-powered railroads were successfully completed. One connected the town of St. Helens with the River Mersey, and the other ran from Parkside to Preston. Enjoying a salary of 650 pounds annually from each railroad, Vignoles had finally attained prosperity as well as professional prominence.

While his two railways in Lancashire were still under construction, Vignoles received an offer to take charge of the building of another short line in Ireland, a proposition that gave him more personal satisfaction than any other he ever received. For more than a decade there had been an acute need for improved transportation facilities between Dublin and the new harbor which the elder John Rennie had constructed in 1816 at Kingstown. Nevertheless, plans to link the city with its harbor by means of a canal failed to materialize because sufficient capital could not be raised on the impoverished island. With the emergence in the late 1820s of steam railroads as a practical and cheaper alternative to canals, Irish promoters naturally turned their thoughts in that direction. A company was organized, funds raised, and the necessary legislation obtained from Parliament during 1831. Shortly after the chartering of the company, the chief engineer died, leaving the project in a precarious situation. The directors then tried to obtain the services of Thomas Telford, and when he declined to take over the Irish railroad, the directors employed George Stephenson to survey the line and make an estimate of the costs of construction. Stephenson and his assistant, Joseph Locke, eventually reported to the directors that £110,000 would be required to build the railroad.

Colonel John Fox Burgoyne, illegitimate son of General Burgoyne of Saratoga fame and Wellington's great engineer, was chairman of the Irish Board of Works, a governmental agency authorized to advance the Dublin railroad company a loan of £75,000. Not being satisfied with Stephenson's plans and estimates, Burgoyne instructed the board's own engineer to prepare separate estimates. As a result, Stephenson was eventually forced out of the post of chief engineer for the Dublin to Kingstown railroad. Burgoyne then arranged for Vignoles, with whom he had been friendly since they had met during the war in Spain, to supersede Stephenson with a salary of £800 a year. Vignoles confided to his diary that the pleasure of replacing the man who had fired him from the L & M railroad was in itself worth at least £1,000.

As in the case of the L & M railroad, the building of the Dublin and Kingstown railway drew as much upon Vignoles' skill as a diplomat as upon his engineering talent. On one hand, he had to satisfy the requirements of the demanding Board of Works; on the other, he had to persuade influential landowners to sell rights of way across their properties, although the parliamentary act chartering the company did not require them to do so. In the first instance, he succeeded so well that he made lifelong personal friends of several key members of the board. In the second, he was able to bring the negotiations for the rights of way to a satisfactory conclusion by employing unorthodox methods. Not only did he offer high prices for the tracts of land involved, but he agreed to construct handsome edifices on the rights-of way which would enhance rather than detract from the adjoining properties. In one case, he promised to erect a decorative iron bridge over the railroad to connect the two pieces of property which had been separated by the railroad. In others, he built a harbor, pier, and fishing and bathing lodges for Lord Cloncurry who owned crucial waterfront property.

The actual construction of the six-mile-long line presented no unusual engineering problem, and it was opened to traffic in 1834. Although Vignoles was already convinced that a flexible foundation for the rails was preferable to the rigid granite roadbed then in vogue, the directors of the company required that he construct the railway on the accepted system. Despite his reservations, Vignoles had to admit that his contractor had produced a very solid smooth roadway. In November 1834 the locomotive "Hibernian" attained the remarkable speed of sixty miles an hour over a short stretch of the line, and a second engine pulling a car containing forty passengers reached a speed of forty-eight miles an hour.

Hoping to publicize the formal opening of the first Irish railroad, Vignoles obtained an audience with the widowed Duchess of Kent with the intention of persuading her and her daughter, Princess Victoria, to be present at the ceremonies. After reminiscing about Vignoles' relations with her late husband, the duchess disappointed the engineer by declining the invitation on the grounds of political complications.

From the day of the opening of the line on December 17, 1834, the company enjoyed a profitable business that exceeded their most optimistic estimates. During the first few years the passenger traffic on the Dublin and Kingstown produced receipts of £2,000 per month (a sum proportionately larger than the earnings of the Liverpool and Manchester railroad, when their different lengths were taken into account), and the stockholders for many years annually received dividends ranging from 5 to 10 per cent.

In 1835 Vignoles was appointed chief engineer for two separate railway projects. One was to be a line connecting Rugby with Derby by way of Leicester to be constructed by the Midland Counties Railway Company. The other was to run from Manchester to Sheffield through a tunnel 5,300 yards long cut through the Pennines. Vignoles completed the first of these lines with his usual dispatch, and the stretch between Nottingham and Derby opened in May 1839. His experience with the Manchester and Sheffield railroad was of an entirely different nature. Errors in judgment brought Vignoles close to financial and professional ruin.[19]

Before naming a chief engineer, the directors of the Sheffield and Manchester Railway Company employed both Vignoles and Joseph Locke, Stephenson's former assistant, to prepare independent surveys of alternative routes. After examining both, the directors selected the route proposed by Vignoles, despite the obvious engineering problems posed by the Pennines tunnel. Vignoles rightly assumed that constructing the tunnel could be the most demanding part of the entire project, and he planned to give it his personal attention. He moved his family into a country residence nearby, and brought his oldest son, Charles, back from Germany, to act as an assistant. Having become emotionally committed to an unusual degree to the building of this railroad, Vignoles invested heavily in the company and persuaded many of his friends to do likewise. Because of the depression of 1837, raising capital proved to be difficult, and it was not until May 1837 that the S & M received its charter from Parliament. Work on the line began in October 1838 with the breaking of ground at one end of the tunnel. Encountering exceptionally hard rock almost immediately, the workmen proceeded slowly. Vignoles underestimated the logistical problems involved in supplying an army of workmen in a very isolated location, and he experienced severe personnel problems as a result.

Because of construction delays and the continuing difficulty in selling shares in the company, the project became endangered. When in 1839 subscriptions were called in by the directors, Vignoles was unable to come forth with the £140,000 for which his purchase of 1,402 shares of stock had obligated him. As a result, he was relieved of his post by the directors, who then sued for that sum in the Court of Exchequer. An adverse judgment handed down by the court in 1843 cost Vignoles £80,000, virtually wiping out all of his financial assets, and leaving him with the necessity of starting over again at the age of fifty. Many friends for whom he had obtained shares in the S & M also suffered heavy losses and some were forced into bankruptcy. The railroad was completed by Locke, who replaced Vignoles as the chief engineer.

During the depression years, 1839–1844, Vignoles struggled desperately to provide for his family by taking any kind of engineering work that came his way, no matter how inconsequential. Once again, Sir John Rennie came to his rescue at a critical moment in 1840, employing him to design a floating pier at the Southwark Iron Bridge. Still having all too much free time on his hands the following year, Vignoles accepted an appointment as professor of civil engineering at University College, the first such professorship in England, and he retained the post for two years. During that period, he delivered during each quarter a series of lectures on the practical aspects of his profession. Meanwhile, he designed an iron slip for the island of St. Thomas. Constructed at Glasgow, the slip was successfully installed in 1843, providing the island with a badly needed harbor. Finally, to his great relief, he was offered that same year an assignment in Europe which was worthy of the attention of a civil engineer of his professional stature.

Resigning his professorship at University College in the spring of 1843, Vignoles went to Germany to prepare plans for a system of state railroads for the kingdom of Württemberg. After a year, he presented the king a set of plans and cost estimates for the railway network. That monarch, however, decided not to adopt Vignoles' proposals. Dismissed with a letter of thanks, a diamond-encrusted snuffbox, and a payment for his services of 2,500 guineas, Vignoles returned to England disappointed at losing an opportunity to build railroads in Germany, but restored professionally and financially. This episode, despite its unfortunate outcome, opened up a new and rewarding phase in Vignoles' career. Henceforth, he was to be largely occupied with major overseas construction projects.

Before taking up his overseas career, Vignoles spent two busy years working on railroads in England and Ireland. In 1845 the return of prosperity to Great Britain released a pent-up mania for the building of new railroads, with no fewer than 300 applications for charters being presented to Parliament in the spring of that year. Civil engineers, after having endured a lean half-decade, suddenly were overwhelmed with opportunities for employment. As one of the better known specialists in railroad engineering, Vignoles had his pick of many projects. To be sure, most of the companies he worked for were unable to obtain parliamentary approval for their schemes, but their political misfortunes reflected no discredit on Vignoles. Even so, several railroads were completed under his direction in Ireland, and in the north and south of England, including the East Kent Railroad (later renamed the London, Chatham, and Dover), the Little Northwestern, and the Waterford and Lemrick in Ireland. In this period Vignoles' rail shaped like an inverted capital T finally won general acceptance in England, years after a similar type had become common on American railroads. This rail, spiked to a longitudinal wooden support, provided a flexible roadway for trains which caused much less damage to rolling stock than the earlier rigid granite-based railway system introduced by Stephenson. Today, the Vignoles rail is regarded as his principal contribution to the development of the British railway system.[20]

For a brief period in the mid-1840s, Vignoles advocated the so-called atmospheric system for propulsion of railway trains in situations where steep grades could not be avoided. Isambard K. Brunel and William Cubitt shared his enthusiasm for the new system, but Stephenson, regarding it as no more than a revival of the stationary engine system, opposed the atmospheric principal vehemently. Again, the unlettered self-made engineer proved to be right when better trained professionals were found to be in error. Between 1846 and 1848 Brunel gave the atmospheric principal a full-scale test on his South Devon line, and ultimately had to concede defeat because no effective means of sealing the slot in the stationary pneumatic tube (through which the train's piston arm moved) could be devised. A leather flap which Brunel employed did permit the passage of the piston arm through the slot, but it failed to make an air-tight seal after the piston and its arm had gone past. Before this crucial test had been conducted by Brunel, Vignoles designed a portion of a railway connecting London with Brighton to operate on the atmospheric system. Because the parent line was not constructed immediately, Vignoles' plan was never given a trial.

While enjoying a welcome rush of business in 1845,

Vignoles was approached by the directors of the East India Company with a proposal that he spend three years in India planning a railway system. Had the offer come a year or two earlier, Vignoles would have accepted without hesitation. As it was, he refused their offer of a salary of £4,000 per annum with an additional thousand pounds for an assistant, and insisted upon £7,000 for himself, £1,000 for an assistant, and transportation costs for both to India and back, with their pay to run from departure to return. When the directors refused to meet his terms, Vignoles rejected their proposal. His arrogant attitude in this instance reveals how greatly his professional circumstances had changed for the better since the loss of his fortune five years earlier. In later years, Vignoles came to regret that he did not undertake the proposed survey for the East India Company, recognizing that he had passed up the opportunity to become the primary railway builder for a subcontinent.

Of all the many foreign construction projects which Vignoles carried out between 1847 and 1865, he was proudest to the end of his life of the great bridge he built across the Dnieper River at Kiev before the Crimean War. Czar Nicholas I for many years had wanted to construct such a bridge at a point where the structure would be protected by his great Kiev fortress, but he could find no engineer who would undertake the project. Upon learning of the czar's interest in the Kiev Bridge from the British consul at Warsaw in 1847, Vignoles decided to apply for the assignment. Drawing up a preliminary plan, he journeyed to St. Petersburg, where he described his proposed bridge to the czar himself. Nicholas was highly pleased with Vignoles' plan and awarded him the contract with the assurance that all of Russia's resources would be put at his disposal. Vignoles surveyed the location at Kiev, and then returned to England to purchase the machines, iron work, and various sophisticated materials which could not be obtained elsewhere.

The construction of the half-mile-long bridge occupied most of Vignoles' time and attention from 1847 to 1853. While designing the bridge, which at the time would be the longest in the world, Vignoles faced several serious problems with which English civil engineers were not familiar. Like the Mississippi River, the Dnieper flowed across a land where bedrock lay very far below the surface. When Vignoles took borings of the bed of the Dnieper, he was dismayed to discover that the bed was composed of an enormously thick layer of sand. He therefore had to design piers which could stand firmly on that insubstantial material. A second engineering problem of even more awesome proportions was caused by an annual change of approximately fifty feet in the water level of the river at Kiev, with a corresponding variation in the velocity of the current. Finally, the spring thaws not only released a mighty surge of water down the Dnieper when the ice broke up, but also sent immense chunks of ice downriver with sufficient velocity to damage bridge piers. During recent decades, spring floods had literally erased all evidence of several earlier attempts to bridge the Dnieper in the region of Kiev.

Finding solutions to these problems was the greatest achievement of Vignoles' career. Having no alternative, he floated his piers on pilings of concrete sunk deeply into the sand of the river bed. In fabricating the pilings, he first built caissons of wooden poles which were driven into the river bed by steam pile drivers. When the caissons were water tight, he dredged out with steam pumps the enclosed water and sand, and filled in the resulting space with concrete. While he was constructing these huge pilings, a spring flood occurred, which presented him with an unanticipated problem that threatened to put an end to his construction project. When the rapidly moving flood of water encountered the bridge caissons, the powerful currents scooped out vast quantities of sand from the bottom of the channels between the obstructions. Vignoles perceived that his pilings would eventually be undermined no matter how deeply he sank them into the river bed. At this juncture, he consulted with Dutch and German engineers who were familiar with this problem. They advised him to protect the foundations of his piers with mattresses filled with stone. Following their advice, Vignoles employed thousands of woodsmen and carpenters to build large box-like structures containing many compartments. These empty boxes were floated into place on the upriver side of the piers and then filled with rock until they sank to the river bed. More rock was then dumped in from the barges moored overhead until the compartments in the mattresses were filled. River currents subsequently cut away at the sand underneath the outer sides of the mattresses until they settled to a permanent position sloping downward at an angle of about forty-five degrees. These slanting mattresses provided such effective protection for the piers, that no change could be detected forty years later.

On top of his five piers, Vignoles built stone towers from the tops of which he suspended the bridge platform, utilizing gigantic wrought-iron chains composed of links twelve feet long. Wrought-iron rods fastened the platform to the chains. When complete in 1853 the Kiev suspension bridge was justly regarded as one of the great engineering feats of the nineteenth century, and Vignoles was acclaimed one of England's eminent civil engineers. Ill luck still continued to dog Vignoles, however. The outbreak of the Crimean War prevented him from receiving payment for building the Kiev bridge until 1857. By then Czar Nicholas had died, and Vignoles was unable to obtain further construction work from his successor. By being away from England for the better part of a decade, Vignoles had also lost his connections with English railroad building, and other and younger railroad engineers had come to the fore.

Vignoles' linguistic and diplomatic skills nevertheless brought him all of the work that he could manage outside of the English-speaking world. Between 1853 and 1855, Vignoles constructed the earliest railway in western Switzerland, a line connecting Lausanne to Morges and Yverdon. Meanwhile, he also became chief engineer on the Frankfort, Wiesbaden, and Cologne Railway. In 1856 Vignoles laid out a Brazilian line connecting Bahia to the San Francisco River, a project finally completed in 1863.

In 1858 Vignoles accepted an appointment as chief engineer of the Tuleda and Bilbao railroad which ran through the mountainous Basque country in Spain. Previously, Spanish engineers had failed to find a workable route, but Vignoles succeeded in surveying a practicable right of way through the mountains. While constructing the line, he had to drive numerous tunnels through the Cantabrian Mountains, including one in which a half-mile of quicksand was encountered. One difficulty, even worse than the tunneling, was resolved only by diverting the Ebro River into another bed, using techniques Vignoles had learned at Kiev.

After the Spanish project was completed, Vignoles entered into a period of semi-retirement. He was connected with railroad building projects on the Isle of Man and in Poland, but most of the responsibility for these assignments were borne by his son Henry, who had worked with him on the Kiev bridge. He retired from professional work completely in 1865, then being seventy-two years old. He died on November 17, 1875.

Vignoles had seven children by his first wife, Mary Griffiths Vignoles (1787–1834), of whom Thomas (1821–1822) and Isabella (1823–1829) perished in early childhood. The oldest son, Charles Ferdinand (1819–?), was educated to be a civil engineer but fell victim to a mental disorder that disabled him permanently. Hutton (1824–?) and Henry (1827–?) Vignoles joined their father's engineering firm upon completing their educations, each becoming a successful civil engineer. Olinthus John Vignoles, M.A. (1829–?), entered the ministry and became assistant-minister at St. Peters Church, Vere Street, London. In addition to his father's biography, Olinthus published a *Memoir of Sir Robert P. Stewart, Kt., Mus. Doc., professor of music in the University of Dublin (1862–94)* (London, 1899). The oldest of the seven children and only surviving daughter, Camilla (who was baptized Anna Hester, by mistake), died unmarried in 1883 at the age of sixty-five. Vignoles' first wife died in Liverpool in 1834, after a long illness, at the age of forty-seven. She was buried in St. James cemetery in that city. Vignoles married a second wife, Elizabeth, in 1849. He had no children during this marriage. Elizabeth survived her husband by five years, dying in 1880. Vignoles, himself, died in Hythe, Hampshire, on November 17, 1875, and was buried in Brompton cemetery, London.

Vignoles received many professional honors during his career. He was elected a member of the Royal Society in 1855, for example, and in 1869 he was chosen president of the Institute of Civil Engineers. Because most of his later working years were spent outside of England, Vignoles is less well known today than many of his contemporaries who had fewer achievements to their credit than Dr. Hutton's irresponsible grandson. Even so, the author of *Victorian Engineering* (1970) counts him among the six greatest civil engineers of nineteenth-century England.[21]

Vignoles' *Observations upon the Floridas* (1823) was one of several works published soon after Spain ceded her East and West Florida provinces to the United States. Among these publications were: [Daniel Blow], *A Geographical, Historical, Commercial, and Agricultural View of the United States; Forming a Complete Emigrant's Directory through Every Part of the Republic; Particularizing the States of Kentucky* ... *East and West Florida* ... (1820) ; [Edward J. Coale], *An Original Memoir on the Floridas, with a General De-*

scription by the Best Authorities, by a Gentleman of the South (1821) ; William Darby, *Memoir on the Geography, and Natural and Civil History of Florida, Attended by a Map of that Country* . . . (1821) ; James Grant Forbes, *Sketches, Historical and Topographical of the Floridas; More Particularly of East Florida* (1821) ; and [William Hayne Simmons], *Notices of East Florida, with an Account of the Seminole Nation of Indians by a Recent Traveller in the Province* (1822).

All of these publications were intended to satisfy the curiosity of Americans about their new territorial acquisition; some were written for the benefit of travelers, and several were brochures of real estate promoters who were trying to lure potential purchasers of Florida lands into their business grasp. The works of Forbes and Vignoles fell into all three categories.

The book about Florida that attracted the most attention at the time of publication, and the one which several generations of historians have considered to be the best description of Florida at the time of its transfer to the United States, was Forbes, *Sketches . . . of the Floridas*. Because the author was a native of East Florida and a United States governmental official in Florida when the book came off the press, his account was considered to be unusually authoritative. Furthermore, Forbes brought out his travel volume about Florida while interest in the new territory was at a peak. Consequently, he was able virtually to monopolize the market.

Forbes was born in St. Augustine in 1769, the son of John Forbes, an influential Anglican clergyman who served on the governor's council throughout the period of the British occupation of Florida. Through his political connections, John Forbes acquired a large land grant which his heirs could not persuade the Spanish authorities to recognize. In 1783 John Forbes went back to England with his family, and his son James was educated there. Upon coming of age, James engaged in business on Santo Domingo for a brief period before settling permanently in the United States. During the War of 1812 Forbes served in the United States Army, rising eventually to the rank of lieutenant colonel. Because Colonel Forbes was known to be familiar with North Florida and because he was experienced in negotiating with Spanish government officials, President Monroe sent him to Cuba in 1821 to arrange the final details of the transfer of Florida to the United States. Upon the successful completion of this mission, Forbes was appointed United States marshal for East and West Florida on the recommendation of General Andrew Jackson, the first territorial governor. Forbes also held the office of mayor of St. Augustine for eighteen months before leaving Florida for New York in late 1822 on account of ill health. He still hoped to obtain a valid title to his father's land grant while he was preparing his *Sketches of the Floridas,* and he intended to use the book as an aid in selling land to settlers.

Although the lengthy historical account with which Forbes began his *Sketches* has been demonstrated to be full of errors, his description of the land and its inhabitants were based largely on his own personal knowledge, and is therefore valuable to historians. While composing his manuscript, he relied on memory rather than on notes or recent observations, so his work is

less specific than that of Vignoles who wrote from detailed descriptions jotted down while on research trips
about East Florida.

Because Charles Vignoles' travel account was published two years later than Forbes' *Sketches* and at a
time of severe economic depression, the book did not
receive nearly as wide a circulation as did Forbes'
work. In one of his letters, Vignoles commented that a
Boston newspaper published a favorable article on his
work, but research has not been able to uncover this
material. Historians also have until recently generally
ignored Vignoles' *Observations*, although Lewis C. Gray
cited Vignoles in his monumental two-volume *History
of Agriculture in the Southern United States to 1860*.[22]
This neglect by scholars has been caused more by a lack
of information about a very rare volume than by mis-
trust of Vignoles' accuracy.

If Vignoles' purpose in writing his *Observations* is
understood, the relative worth of any particular part of
his commentary is readily apparent to the reader. The
book was intended to be a supplement to Vignoles' new
map of Florida, which the author considered to be his
more important contribution. Having been engaged for
several years in charting the coastline of South Carolina, Vignoles was keenly aware that the existing maps
of the waters off the South Atlantic states were dan-
gerously inadequate for navigational purposes. He was
convinced that northeast Florida would gain population
very rapidly in the near future, and he assumed that
water transportation by sea and river would be vital to
the newcomers. Hence, he focused his attention as a
map-maker on the northeastern coast of Florida; this

was where he expected sea-borne commerce to expand
in the immediate future. Employing a large rowboat, he
charted the shoreline and the larger streams that flowed
into the Atlantic, and recorded observations about the
characteristics of the lands bordering the ocean and
the streams. In addition, he undertook trips on horse-
back into the hinterland of East Florida to determine
the suitability of the various regions for agriculture.
Finally, he traveled by sea to the southern tip of the
peninsula of Florida, although his observations of the
southeastern coast necessarily were more superficial
than in the north.[23]

As a trained surveyor and military engineer, Vignoles had a keen eye for topography and natural resources, but he was comparatively indifferent to Florida
society in all but its economic aspects. He had little to
say about the Indians, and he wasted few words on
descriptions of the towns. What he did produce was a
reliable guide for persons traveling by water and land
about East Florida, to which he added as much information as he could obtain from other sources about
those parts of Florida with which he was not particularly familiar. He also attempted to round out his
Observations by including some information about English and Spanish land grants, for this was a subject
that would concern immigrants interested in purchasing Florida lands. He admitted frankly, however,
that his information about this subject was based on
questionable sources.

While preparing his commentary to accompany his
map, Vignoles went to unusual pains to make clear to
a reader which parts were based on personal knowl-

edge, which parts were derived from interviews with local residents, and which parts were extracted from written sources. Modern readers can rely implicitly on statements for which Vignoles himself is the authority, because he strove for the same standard of accuracy that he used in making mathematical computations. Throughout his long career, Vignoles was transparently honest in all of his transactions. The same quality permeates his *Observations upon the Floridas*.

JOHN HEBRON MOORE.

The Florida State University.

NOTES.

1. Unless indicated otherwise, biographical information about Charles B. Vignoles was derived from a biography written by his son, Olinthus J. Vignoles, *Life of Charles Blacker Vignoles* (London, 1889). Olinthus Vignoles used his father's journals and letters as his principal sources, but also did extensive research in the British Museum, the Institute of Civil Engineers, and in the archives of several British railroads with which his father had been associated. He indicated that his father's letters and journals were in the possession of a younger brother, Henry Vignoles. O. J. Vignoles published excerpts from a few letters and described the remainder of the material from the Florida period of his father as being scanty. Biographical sketches of Charles B. Vignoles are in the *Dictionary of National Biography* (*DNB*), s.v. "Vignoles, Charles Blacker"; N. W. Webster, *Joseph Locke: Railway Revolutionary* (London, 1970), pp. 42–44, 105–9. References to Vignoles are in [William Hayne Simmons], *Notices of East Florida* (Charleston, S.C., 1822; facsimile ed., introduction by George E. Buker, Gainesville, Fla., 1973), pp. 22, 24; James Kip Finch, *Story of Engineering* (New York, 1960), p. 218; Samuel Smiles, *Life of George Stephenson and His Son Robert Stephenson* (New York, 1868), pp. 279, 291, 311.

2. The history of the British military campaign in the Windward Islands, during which Vignoles' father and mother perished, is in Bryan Edwards, *History, Civil and Commercial, of the British Colonies in the West Indies*, 4 vols. (Philadelphia, 1806), 4:287–310; J. W. Fortescue, *History of the British Army*, 2nd ed., 13 vols. (London, 1915), 4:350–84.

3. For references to Victor Hugues, see Edwards, *History of the British Colonies in the West Indies*, 4:306–7; Sir Harry Johnston, *The Negro in the New World* (New York, 1969), pp. 168–69; Henry Leméry, *La Révolution Française à la Martinique* (Paris, 1936), pp. 292–98; John H. Parry and Philip M. Sherlock, *A Short History of the West Indies*, 3rd ed. (London, 1971), p. 171; Alexandre Moreau de Jonnes, *Adventures in Wars of the Republic and Consulate* (London, 1920), pp. 118–20; P. Levot, *Histoire de la ville et du port de Brest pendant la Terreur* (Brionne, 1971), pp. 154–73, 181–213; Fortescue, *History of the British Army*, 4:370; Thomas Ott, *The Haitian Revolution, 1789–1804* (Knoxville, Tenn., 1973), p. 86; Vignoles, *Charles Blacker Vignoles*, p. 7.

4. *DNB*, s.v. "Hutton, Charles"; Vignoles, *Charles Blacker Vignoles*, pp. 6–7.

5. *DNB*, s.v. "Hutton, Charles"; Vignoles, *Charles Blacker Vignoles*, pp. 5, 8–15.

6. Fortescue, *History of the British Army*, 4:chap. 17.

7. R. Money Barnes, *The Scottish Regiments* (London, 1956), p. 126.

8. Ibid., pp. 129–30.

9. *DNB*, s.v. "MacGregor, Sir Gregor."

10. Charleston (S.C.) *Courier*, January 23, November 3, 1821.

11. Ibid., January 3, 1822.

12. Clarence E. Carter, ed., *Territorial Papers of the United States*, 28 vols. (Washington, 1933–76), 22:360.

13. Bell was at the time acting secretary and acting governor of East Florida. The Vignoles materials are in the National Archives (War Department, CE, Bulky File No. 40). See Carter, *Territorial Papers*, 22:754.

14. Copies of the Vignoles map of Florida are in both the National Archives and in the Library of Congress. In the National Archives, one is filed as Ref. Coll.: Florida 1823; another is filed as L69 in RG 77. Photocopies are available in Florida, including the Robert Strozier Library, Florida State University, Tallahassee.

15. Vignoles' prospectus was published in the Charleston (S.C.) *Courier*, July 22, 1822, as follows:

A NEW MAP OF FLORIDA

Early in October, will be published, A New Map of Florida, compiled from recent actual surveys and observations, and also from authentic documents, made and collected during a residence in that country.

To accompany the Map, but for the public convenience issued separately, at the same time, *Observations Upon the Floridas*, from original notes taken during several journies [sic] in the interior, particularly through parts hitherto unexplored, and information drawn from the most authentic sources,

By Charles Vignoles,

Civil and Topographical Engineer, lately of South Carolina; and at present a resident Surveyor of East Florida.

The Map will be about 26 inches square, delineated on a scale of 20 miles to the inch; the whole of the principal and almost all the tributary water courses and the chief lakes will be laid down; the existing carriage roads and all the main Indian paths, the names of places of entertainment, &c. will be noted—the local appellations being carefully retained to avoid confusion, as it will be an object to render the Map as convenient and useful as possible to travellers; independent of the general details, all large grants of lands will be located as far as is practicable.

The accompanying book will contain a review of the state of the province in a statistical and civil light, for a few years previous to and at the time of its Cession.

A summary description of the country in general as respects soil, climate and topographical details, with remarks on the different appropriate cultures, particularly coffee, sugar, Cuban tobacco and fruit.

An abstract as far as is obtainable of all the grants made by the Spanish authorities in the Floridas, with the names of the original grantees, &c. explanations of the principal [sic] upon which lands were generally conceded, and an account of the different laws, royal orders &c. authorizing the Gouvernors to make grants.

Such information respecting the Indians, the wrecking systems among the Keys and Reefs, and other general points as they may be considered useful or interesting to the public.

The price will be made as low as possible, it being presumed that the Map and Pamphlet may be issued at a sum not exceeding $3 for both. Names of Subscribers for the Map and Book will be received at this Office until the 1st September next, and the copies will be accordingly forwarded as soon as published, payable on delivery.

St. Augustine, June 29, 1822.

16. The Library of Congress lists a work by Vignoles entitled *The History of the Floridas, from the discovery by Cabot in 1497, to the cession of the same to the United States, in 1821. With observations on the climate, soil and productions.* By Charles Vignoles . . . Brooklyn, N.Y. Printed by G. L. Birch, 1824. Birch, 99 Fulton Street, Brooklyn, N.Y., was the printer who produced the 1823 version which was published by E. Bliss & E. White, 128 Broadway. Very likely Vignoles owed Birch money which the latter tried to recoup by selling the book under a title better calculated to attract purchasers. He may have done this with or without Vignoles' approval.

17. Webster, *James Locke*, pp. 40–44; Smiles, *George and Robert Stephenson*, pp. 254–323.

18. Webster, *James Locke*, pp. 42–43; Vignoles, *Charles Blacker Vignoles*, pp. 111–20.

19. Webster, *James Locke*, pp. 105–10; Vignoles, *Charles Blacker Vignoles*, pp. 233–44.

20. *Encyclopedia Britannica*, 11th ed., s.v. "Railways".

21. Lionel T. C. Rolt, *Victorian Engineering* (London, 1970), p. 23.

22. Lewis C. Gray, *History of Agriculture in the Southern United States to 1860*, 2 vols. (Gloucester, Mass., 1958), 2:901.

23. Not everyone agreed as to the accuracy of Vignoles' map. In a letter to the secretary of war, dated September 29, 1823, written at St. Augustine, James Gadsden wrote: "Little confidence is to be placed in the accuracy of Vignoles' map—as to the Interior of the Country; the Sea Coast may be correct as he had resort to some of the best English & Spanish Charts—The interior of Florida has never been explored. that I can ascertain— Vignoles made but a short excursion into the Country West of St. Augustine—He never was more than 20 miles South of Alachua—The position of Okahumky & other Indian villages as laid down by him is grossly erroneous." Carter, *Territorial Papers*, 22:754.

OBSERVATIONS

UPON

THE FLORIDAS.

OBSERVATIONS

UPON

THE FLORIDAS.

BY
CHARLES VIGNOLES,
CIVIL AND TOPOGRAPHICAL ENGINEER.

NEW-YORK:

PUBLISHED BY E. BLISS & E. WHITE, 128 BROADWAY.

1823.

G. L. Birch, Printer, 99 Fulton-street, Brooklyn.

CONTENTS.

INTRODUCTORY OBSERVATIONS.

THE newly acquired territory of Florida has advanced the soil of the Union to the very verge of the tropics, and by placing the ports from the mouths of the Mississippi round to Amelia island, under the American flag, has hermetically closed all approaches to our interior. The various political advantages arising from the cession have been often set forth, and are too well appreciated to require enumeration in a pamphlet of topographical details. The country has singularities and advantages in various points of view, which. at a remoter period, may be estimated with impartiality, and found to be of importance.

The following observations upon the Floridas have been collected, during a residence in the country; in which period several extensive journeys were made, with a view of obtaining materials for the construction of a new map, and for the purpose now brought forward. Some reports sent to the Indian department, at the seat of government, copies of which appeared in one of the Boston papers, contain a few of the results of the author's personal observations, and make the basis of these notes, though now modified, and in several parts changed, from the acquisition of better information. Those who may peruse these pages must not expect the glowing narrative of an agreeable excursion, through regions comparable to a paradise. The subsequent relation has only truth to recommend it, and from the very nature of the work, must appear dry and tedious to all not immediately interested in the resources of the territory. It will be observed that a fuller account is given of the Atlantic border than of the Mexican shore; its evident pre-importance, on some accounts, led naturally to the earliest examination, and the many excellencies it possesses encouraged investigation, which the nature of the coast, and its nearer vicinity to recourses, rendered more practicable; added to which the author's domicile at St. Augustine, and the total ignorance of a country so comparatively near the capital, induced him to explore and remark personally; and in consequence it may be noted, that on the map almost the whole sea-

coast from St. Mary's river to cape Florida, is from
his own actual survey; the names of places are set down
as best known to the very few residents in the vicinity, and the traveller or shipwrecked mariner may rely
upon the general accuracy of the detail. The fabulous reports of the inland bays, lakes and waters,
which have heretofore existed, respecting the southern part of the Florida peninsula, will be readily accounted for, on a view of the map, and a glance at
the description of what is there actually to be found.

It is lamented that no account sufficiently satisfactory could be procured upon West Florida; the complete separation of the two divisions of the territory
from all communication with each other, and the total
impracticability of the author's extending his enquiries
to that portion of the country, have been the occasion
of this defect. Enough, however, is to be gleaned
from former accounts to infer, that the soil and climate
is not materially different from the adjacent lands in
the Mississippi and Alabama territories. The able
editor of the paper published at Pensacola, laments
himself the dearth of topographical and statistical information, and has made his appeal to the few scattered inhabitants to supply the defect; but it has
not been ascertained whether if with any and what
success, the appeal has been answered. Called by
his professional duties, it was not in the author's pow-

er to make an actual inspection of all the points he
attempts to describe ; but he is under the conviction
that his authorities are respectable, and he has not
relied, except upon concurrent testimony, from more
than one creditable source.

In sketching the civil history of the province for the
few years preceding the cession to the United States,
the author is almost wholly indebted to the valuable manuscripts of George I. F. Clarke, Esq. surveyor
general of East Florida, and lieutenant-governor
of the northern district of that province, while under
the dominion of Spain. This gentleman, whose information on this and every other subject connected
with the country, is very extensive, furnished with a
peculiar urbanity every assistance ; and likewise some
of the remarks on the Indians. The friendly assistance
and judicious hints afforded by N. A. Ware, Esq. one
of the commissioners of land claims, call for especial
acknowledgments; indeed the present map and pamphlet were first put into a train of publication at his
suggestion, and by his striking out the general ideas
upon it. In the observations on the keys and reefs
of the Florida point, the information of the resident
pilots at the cape, have been chiefly relied on, as
they were corroborated by the accounts of several
masters of vessels, particularly Captain Snyder of
New-York, who have navigated among them, and do
not differ from the directions of Romans, De Brahm

and their co-temporaries, who have been fully consulted and abstracted, as far as they were considered useful.

It had always been a particular wish of the author to have given a list of all the grants upon record, but not having been able to obtain permission to search the archives, after the departure to Pensacola of the honourable Edmund Law, who had previous to that period the charge of them, he must confine himself to general accounts. He has located upon the map as many of the large grants as have come within his knowledge, but as he has no official information on the subject of any of them, they must be understood as having been laid down, solely with a view of gratifying the general existing desire of knowing, where the larger concessions lay, and their relative position to each other.

In constructing the map of Florida, the author has availed himself of all the existing charts and maps, both domestic and foreign of all nations, as well as of various manuscript draughts. Among those consulted, were Romans' chart of Florida, the British nautical survey of West Florida, from the mouths of the Mississippi to the embouchure of the Suwanee, the royal Spanish chart of the gulf of Mexico, from the marine depot at Madrid, and various other Spanish maps, Ellicott's map attached to his journal, while running the Florida line, Gault's survey of the Florida keys, and a variety of other charts of the coast. Among the manuscripts made use of were ; Sketches of the river Saint John, partly from the author's own drawing, and the rest furnished by Peter Mitchel, Esq. corrected by a sight of Capt. Le Conte's accurate survey of the whole of that interesting river from its mouth up to the the very head lake, and a very correct British manuscript chart of St. John's river, from the bar to the Cowford ; the author's own survey of the coast from St. Augustine to cape Florida, extending to the heads of all the waters on the Atlantic border ; but his best assistance more particularly for the interior of West Florida, was from the manuscript map drawn by the late Jos. Purcell, Esq. formerly of S. Carolina, which is now in the topographical bureau at Washington, to which, with a liberality and attention never to be forgotten, the author was allowed access for the purposes of his map ; this document contained the results of all that was known to the British government up to the time of the re-cession of the Floridas by Great Britain to Spain. The boundary line as lately run by Georgia, was furnished me by the politeness of the Surveyor General of that state ; Saint Mary's River, from the manuscript survey of Zephaniah Kingsley, Esq. an enlightened and valuable citizen of Florida ; Nassau river and Dunn's lake, from surveys made under the direction

of Mr. Turnbull, a great proprietor in the Territory.
The author's journeys in the interior, assisted by the
valuable notes and information of Peter Mitchell, Esq.
enabled him to fill up the detail from the old path to
fort St. Marks, to the head waters of Tampa bay and
across, along that parallel to the Atlantic. The remainder is filled in by the information derived from
Lewis, Hegan and Pent, respectable pilots at cape
Florida, who mentioned the names of various persons,
still living in the Bahamas, who had travelled therein, and by the unanimous testimony of every indian
and indian negro consulted on the subject. Mr. Lewis, his father and family, lived for many years on various parts of the western coast, from the mouth of the
Suwanee, down to Cape Romano, and he afforded me
much local information.

After all, I am aware the map is not perfect, but it
concentrates all that is at present known of the territory; and if, where information was wholly unattain-
able, no directions can be given to the traveller or
new settler, yet he may be assured that where the
detail *is* laid down, that it is accurate and will not
mislead him. Sensible of all possible respect for the
opinions of an enlightened public, the work is offered
to them, with all its imperfections on its head; but
conscious that some account was desirable of Florida,
the author has in the following pages, and upon the

map, used his humble endeavors to collect facts and describe realities. Should his attempt to afford a better knowledge of this new country fail, he hopes the candor of his judges will attribute it to any thing but want of exertions, and pardon a futile essay, which was at least founded on good intentions.

———

Since the manuscript of this work was completed, the accounts from East Florida, respecting the sugar cane, have been uncommonly favorable: several large establishments are about to be erected, and considerable investments are making for the express purpose of raising the cane. It is a matter of infinite satisfaction, that the certainty of sugar becoming the *staple* of Florida is already established : let us hope that the success in this article, will induce other not less certain sources of wealth to be explored. The olive, the grape, the silk-worm, and many more which are detailed under their proper head, are equally worthy the attention of the agriculturist.

On the subject of the territorial government we have reason to believe, that by the exertions of the delegate from Florida; Joseph M. Hernandez, Esq. the east and west divisions will be placed under separate administrations and a separate board of commissioners, appointed for each province ; by which means all existing difficulties will be smoothed and the hold- ers of titles enabled without difficulty or expense to establish their claims, and settlers will pour in from all parts of the union to enjoy the advantages so liberal- ly bestowed by nature upon Florida.

The map of Florida which is published at the same time with this book, by the author, will for the accommodation of the public, be sold, either bound up with it, or separately in sheets, done up in cases or mounted and varnished, with roller, colored or uncolored as required

HISTORICAL OBSERVATIONS.

—————

FLORIDA was discovered in the year 1497, by Cabot; but it does not appear that the country was either named or explored until fifteen years afterwards, when Don Juan Ponce de Leon landed, in April, 1512, and finding the earth covered with a luxuriant vegetation, in *flower*, he styled the new region *Florida*, or *Florida Blanca*. It was visited a few years afterwards by Narvaez, and many other adventurers ; and in 1538, Ferdinand de Soto, so cele-brated in antient books of travels, disembarked an army in Spirito Santo Bay, and marched through the interior, fighting the Indians and destroying his troops, without gaining a single point ; and after traversing round to the Missisippi, died at the end of three or four years, near the mouth of the Red river. His narrative throws but little light on the real state of the country, and at present is looked upon as a mere historical romance ; for though he doubtless actually passed through the places he describes, yet with a view to palliate his lavish waste of life to the Spanish government, he has interwo-ven fabulous accounts of gold, pearls and treasures, which never existed. The first colony in Florida was planted in 1562, by Ribault, a Frenchman, near the mouth of the river Saint John ;

3

but the unfortunate Protestants, who had fled from persecution in Europe, found the vindictive spirit of bigotry follow, and in 1564, Menendez exterminated them with a demoniac malignity, unequalled by the horrors of the fatal festival of Saint Bartholomew in their own country. Dominique de Gorgues, in 1568, took ample revenge, and hung the murderers on the same branches from which depended the bleached skeletons of his compatriots.

Saint Augustine appears to have been built about 1565, and is undoubtedly the oldest town on the continent of North America, except the Mexican settlements. At the time this town was evacuated in 1763, by the Spaniards, one at least of the original houses remained, with the date of 1571 upon the front, and all were without chimnies or glass windows. Sir Francis Drake, in 1586, pillaged the town; a ceremony repeated by the Indians in 1611 : and in 1665 Captain Davis, in the piratical spirit of the times, once more desolated the place, which, from these checks, and other causes, does not appear to have much advanced in size or population. Governor Moore of South Carolina, made a fruitless attack upon the fort at Saint Augustine in 1702; and in 1725, Colonel Palmer of Georgia, was equally unsuccessful. General Ogelthorpe, with a large force from Savannah, was completely repulsed in 1740, and retreated in disorder. At length the peace of 1763 gave the Floridas to Great Britain, and for the subsequent twenty years Saint Augustine appears greatly to have improved. The author has conversed with many persons who were there in June 1784, when it again reverted to Spain, and has heard them speak highly of the beauty of the gardens, the neatness of the houses, and the air of cheerfulness and comfort that seemed, during that preceding period, to have been thrown over the town. Neglect and consequent decay, attended this interesting town during its occupancy by the Spaniards ; where time or equinoctial storms damaged any buildings, public or private, the hand of repair never came, and at the period of the cession, this once elegant place appeared ruinous, dirty, and unprepossessing.

Pensacola appears to have been founded some time previous to 1696 ; it was in that year taken from the French by Riola, and in 1699, Monsieur D'Iberville failed in his attempt to retake it. In 1719, it was three times taken and retaken, and at length retained by France ; but in 1722 was restored to Spain. The prosperity of Pensacola and decay seems to have been somewhat similar to its sister city. The history of Florida is not the subject of this publication, and the preceding paragraphs have merely been drawn out to refresh the memory of the reader, who will find in various modern publications more minute information ; but as some interest has been excited to learn the real state of affairs as connected with East Florida, for a few years previous to and at the time of the cession, the author is happy in being able to gratify the public wish. Sometime in the summer of 1811, general Mathews appears, in consequence of an act of congress passed in the preceding session, to have been authorised by the executive to proceed to the frontiers of Georgia, to accept possession of East Florida from the local authorities, or to take it against the attempt of a foreign power to occupy it, holding it in either case subject to future and friendly negotiation. This act appears to have been passed in consequence of the revolution which had just broken out in the northern district of East Florida. This official appearance of American interference, alarmed the government of St. Augustine, who appear to have appealed to the British minister at Washington, who accordingly expostulated with Mr. Monroe, then secretary of state. General Mathews appears in his zeal to carry the orders of the executive into effect, to have exceeded his powers, indeed it has been confidently asserted that the insurrection was fostered by his appearance. His taking possession of Amelia Island and other parts of East Florida, was officially blamed, and his commission revoked in April, 1812, and the governor of

Georgia was commissioned in his place, in consequence, as the official letter states, of general Mathews having employed the troops of the United States, to dispossess the Spanish authorities by force : ordering a restoration of Amelia Island and other parts to the Spanish authorities—stipulating for the protection of such inhabitants as had joined the Americans from the anger of the Spanish government. A later letter states, that if the troops are to be withdrawn that governor Mitchell is not to interfere, to compel the patriots to deliver the country to the Spanish authorities.

The following letters will carry a true idea of the general history of that part of the country.

[COPY.]

St. Augustine, 25th July, 1821.

Capt. John R. Bell, Commanding the province of East Florida.

Sir,

The following is intended to comply with your desire of information on the northern division of this province ; and in order to your comprehending the true state of that section, and the character of its inhabitants, to whom, as the officer that presided over them for the last five years, I feel grateful for their confidence, their devotion, and their support, permit me to recapitulate a part of its history ; and first to premise : that it is bounded on the north by Camden county, Georgia, the southernmost part of the Atlantic states ; the river St. Mary, the line of demarcation, and a very narrow one, has long been the "jumping place" of a large portion of the bad characters who gradually sift through the whole southwardly : warm climates are congenial to bad habits. Second, that, unfortunately for Florida, the laws of both governments had the effect of making each country the asylum of the bad men of the other ; consequently, Florida must have received, we will suppose, twenty of those for one it returned to Georgia. This must be the result, on taking only a numerical view of the population of the two countries.

And thirdly, that by the orders of the Spanish court, prohibiting citizens of the United States from being received as settlers in Florida, the only part from whence it was ever to expect a population sufficiently large to make it respectable, the good were prevented from coming in, while the bad must come. The result of an observation, perhaps inadvertent, made in congress long since, *Florida must ultimately be ours, if only from emigration*, and loudly commented on by the Spanish minister.

The revolution, commenced in March, 1812, had spread general desolation and ruin over the whole province; the dust of a siege had been thirteen months snuffed within the walls of St. Augustine. On the 6th May, 1813, the assailants were withdrawn, and the town of Fernandina was restored to the Spanish authorities.

The Spanish government had published a general pardon to its subjects, but, unfortunately, had limited it to three months, a time too short for the ebullitions of individual feelings to subside. Many, and those of the most energetic and influential character, would not trust themselves among the opposite party. The time expired, and those were consequently left out. And in August, of the same year, hostilities re-commenced; more sanguinary scenes ensued; and the insurgents aided by bands of idlers from Georgia, took and kept possession of all the territory lying to the west and north of St. John's river. Fernandina having become too weak for offence, and St. Augustine not being willing to let out all its troops, to hunt " bush fighters," the newly styled *Republic of Florida*, over which the influence of order had not been felt since March, 1812, and having now no compulsive inducement to union among its members, soon fell into the most wretched state of anarchy and licentiousness; even the honest were compelled to knavery in their own defence, and thus continued until August, 1816—while the most rancorous feelings were bandied between the " Pat-Riots" of the main, and the " damn'd Spaniards" of Amelia island.

At that period preparations were making on the ~~Maine~~ *main* for a descent on Fernandina, then too weak to stand even on the defensive, and no succors were to be expected from our friends, nor was there any thing like good quarters to be looked for from our enemies. Governor Coppinger had lately received the command of the province. I knew his energetic and benevolent character ; that his discretionary powers were very great, but his want of means, deplorable ; and I personally knew the people of the main, and had had in other days, influence among them. I proposed a plan of reconciliation and re-establishment of order. It was patronized by the governor, and I received orders to proceed according to circumstances. Messrs. Zephaniah Kingsley and Henry Yonge went with me up St. Mary's river to Mills' ferry, and met about forty of them, and after much debate an agreement for a general meeting at Waterman's Bluff in three weeks, was concluded on.

The day of meeting arrived, and none others but the gentlemen I have mentioned would leave Fernandina. We knew that nothing short of an election of officers would subdue those people, even should they be willing to submit to order at all ; and that was a course opposite to the principles of the Spanish government. However, extraordinary cases require extraordinary remedies ; and circumstances authorising a long stride, I provided several copies of a set of laws adapted to their circumstances, blank commissions, instructions, &c. A gathering of several hundred, besides a crowd of spectators from Georgia, met us at the place appointed, a mere mob without head or leader. I tendered them a distribution into three districts of all the territory lying between St. John's river and St. Mary's, with a magistrate's court and a company of militia in each ; and those to be called Nassau, Upper and Lower St. Mary's ; an election of officers from the mass of the people of each, without allowing the candidates to offer themselves ; that the officers to be elected should be immediately commissioned to enter on the functions of their offices ; and that all the past should be buried in total oblivion. These were received by a general expression of satisfaction ; a table was brought out on the green, and in a few hours a territory containing about one half of the population of East Florida was brought to order ; three magistrates and nine officers of militia elected, commissioned, instructed and provided with laws. Every demonstration of satisfaction ensued ; they took up their officers on their shoulders, hailed by the shouts of hundreds. A plentiful feast and many interesting scenes of friendship and mirth closed the important day.

His excellency approved of the proceedings, and tendered me a superintending jurisdiction on the whole, which I admitted, on his consenting to strike out Amelia island : that had a commandant who had a plenty of leisure to attend to the complaints of Fernandina, and I have ever since allowed them the election of officers in filling up vacancies.

Such have been the confidence and resignation of those people, that all complaints and appeals that should have gone before the superior courts at St. Augustine, have been referred to me for an opinion, and those opinions have ever been voluntarily conclusive, to any amount. And such their devotion to the government, that at the shortest notice, any part or the whole force of the three districts have met me at the place appointed, mounted, armed and victualled, each at his own expense.

Three facts speak volumes in favor of those inhabitants :—First, that in five years there has not been one appeal and but one complaint to the superior authorities, in St. Augustine, although the high road to both has all the while been open. Second, that Georgians prefer suing Floridians in that part of Florida to suing them in Georgia. Third, that the credit of Floridians stands higher in Georgia than ever it did before, from whence they get all their supplies. Such is the deplorable state of human nature, that a robbery or a murder will occur in the best regulated societies ; within a fortification ; but I can venture to assert, that in no part of the civilized world do fewer irregularities occur among so many inhabitants, than in the northern division of this province.

I would caution, that when the people of Florida are spoken of with censure, some regard would be paid to the person speaking, as to who he is, or from whence he gets his information ; to the period to which reference is had, and the part of Florida alluded to. I am aware that the time has been when these were censurable, for they were above four years in a state of anarchy ; the broadside of their country open to the idle and vicious of Georgia ; and even after they were called to order, in 1816, some time was required for purification, by compelling many to decamp, and others to mend their manners. And on the other side of St. John's river, under another local jurisdiction, many who were hunted out from the northern division found toleration.

We knew that a practice called Lynch's law had done more good in Georgia in a few months, before Florida was found to be an asylum for the vicious, than the civil authority could have done in as many years in that part of the country ; and we were aware that some such energetic measure was indispensible to accelerate our purification. Fines, floggings and banishment, therefore, became the penalties for all wilful injury committed on the property of another, not as a law of Spain, but as a special compact of the people. A man who stole his neighbor's cow, was tried by a congress of from twenty to thirty persons of his district, summoned for the purpose, and on being clearly convicted, he was sentenced to receive, tied to a pine tree, from ten to thirty-nine lashes ; and that was executed on the spot, by each giving him two lashes, to the amount of his sentence ; and the second offence of the same class was punished by flogging and banishment from those districts. A few such examples firmly managed, and executed under the rifles selected from a company, drawn up for the purpose, (and but few were required) did us more good than a board of lawyers, and a whole wheel-barrow of law books could have done.

A mere remonstrance was sufficient to reduce to a small amount, on our side of St. Mary's river, the very grievous evil of parties of Floridians and Georgians combined, going frequently to the indian country of Florida to plunder cattle ; a lucrative practice that had been going on for years, and was carried to such excess, that large gangs of cattle could be purchased along that river, at the low price of from two to three dollars per head. Efforts to suppress it altogether, we found to be in vain, without a suitable coincidence on the Georgia side ; and experience had shown that the civil authority was too heavy booted to make much impression on those " moggasin boys." I then wrote to general Floyd, who commanded a part of the Georgia militia, and his prompt and efficient aid soon enabled us to put a finishing stroke to a practice replete with the worst of evils.

When general M'Gregor got possession of Fernandina, he was in the belief that he had conquered Florida to the walls of St. Augustine, and that there was nothing more to be done, as related to these people, but display his standard, fill up his ranks, and march to the possession ; and under that impression he brought several sets of officers. But neither the offers, threats nor intrigues of himself and his successors, Irvin, Hubbard and Aury, and their many friends in many places, could bring one of them to his flag. Whereas, when a call was made for volunteers to commence in advance the expedition formed in St. Augustine, for the re-capture of Amelia island, every man turned out, well equipped, not excepting the superannuated. We got possession of all Amelia island to the very town of Fernandina, and kept it for several days awaiting the troops from St. Augustine. During that time twenty-seven of these men sought for, gave battle to, drove from the field, and pursued to within the range of the guns of Fernandina, above one hundred of M'Gregor's men,

4

with the loss of seven killed and fourteen wounded, and without having lost one drop of blood on our side ; leaving us to bury their dead. The reverses that afterwards attended that expedition were wholly to be attributed to the conduct of the commanding officer who arrived from St. Augustine.

When the constitutional government was ordered in Florida, a few months since, some small alteration were made in the laws of those districts. They were but small, for the laws handed them in 1816 were principally bottomed on the same constitutional government, which had been in force in this province in 1813 and 14. But the administration of St. Augustine having been pleased to form the whole province, about fifty thousand square miles, into one parish, making that city the centre, so far defalcated what those people conceived their constitutional rights, that they petitioned government ; and not getting what they expected, they had in meditation to send a representative to the captain-general of Cuba, and further should it be necessary, when the near approach of the surrender of the province to the United States levelled all dissentions.

Those three districts contain about one half of the population of East Florida, say about fifteen hundred souls, and embrace three fourths of the agricultural interest of the whole province. They are very thinly settled, and form one of the most inferior sections of Florida, as relates to good lands, and indeed many other natural advantages. The causes that have congregated so large a portion of the industrious part of the population into one of the least delectable sections, are these : Its vicinity to Georgia, a populous country, bordering on the river St. Mary, a near and ready market for their produce and their supplies, and the facility of avoiding duties of exports and imports ; the occupancy or neighborhood of Indians in better sections ; the want of protections ; the want of a population sufficient to protect itself ; and revolutionary broils with government, forced upon us by foreigners in their over-strained assi-

duity for our welfare, gagging us with freedom, the most free, civilized people perhaps in the world, and would fain lately have put
it down our throats with negroes' bayonets. [Vide the Jenett, the
Mathews, and the McGregor invasions, in 1794, 1812, and 1817.]

East Florida was literally evacuated by the British, when delivered to the Spanish authorities in 1784. Perhaps no such other general emigration of the inhabitants of a country, amicably transferred
to another government, ever occurred. Spain allowed it many extraordinary privileges, such as were not enjoyed by any other part
of her dominions, and continued augmenting them ever since. In
1792, Florida was opened to a general emigration, without exception of country or creed; and it was rapidly progressing to importance, when the report of the Spanish minister I have mentioned,
closed the gates against American citizens, some time about 1804,
and virtually shut us in from the world as to a large population.

The decline of this province must be dated from that period, in
which a very large portion of the convulsions of Europe necessarily
fell to the share of Spain, from her contiguity to imperial France,
and which called her attentions and resources to objects of more
consideration. But that decline was graduated by the nature of
things to a slow progression, and we had other fair prospects in our
favour, notwithstanding the prohibition of a population from the United States, when the troubles of 1812 spread, in one year, universal
ruin. The war between the United States and Great Britain, and
the visit of McGregor, following in close succession, almost every
one, who had the means of migrating, abandoned a country so much
and so unmeritedly affected.

Your obedient servant,
GEO. I. F. CLARKE.

[COPY.]

Circular to the officers and people of the northern division of East Florida.

ST. MARY'S, FLORIDA, 13th August, 1821.

John Low, Esq. Magistrate of the lower district of St. Mary's.

DEAR SIR,

I take the earliest opportunity afforded me since my return from St. Augustine, to communicate the following :

The authorities of the United States having received possession of this province, on the 10th of last month, my functions as superintending officer of the northern division of East Florida, and those of surveyor-general of the province, have ceased ; and my claims on the Spanish government do not permit my receiving, at present, official charges under the present government. I have not however taken my leave of you all, nor of my former residence : a reciprocity of grateful feelings, happily experienced for the last five years, forbid my doing so. I have therefore promised captain Bell, who now commands this province, who has your welfare warmly at heart, and with whose amiable disposition you will be well pleased, that my every aid and assistance, ex-officio, shall be cheerfully employed for your good.

While in St. Augustine, I laid before captain Bell, a long and candid statement of these districts ; a character of these people that I trust will ensure them the consideration of their new government ; copies of which will be transmitted to the executive of the United States, to general Jackson, and remain in Florida as a record of their merit.

It was to me a pleasing task ; a tribute due to their devotion to their country, and to the confidence and support I have all along experienced from them. Where but in this division of Florida can it be said, that no part of half the population of a province have, in five years, made an appeal, or a complaint, to superior authority residing at hand, and the high road for both always open? Where but in the same division can it be said, that foreigners prefer suing the people of the country in their own courts, to suing them in theirs, where they have them frequently in their power? Where but in this meritorious division can it be said, that any part of, or the whole physical force of three districts, have never failed to meet, at the earliest notice, and that cheerfully, to execute any orders given, armed, mounted and victualled, each at his own expense, and without pay?

An active, brave, hardy, and hospitable people. A people, who having been compromised and thrown into anarchy and confusion, by foreign bayonets, and remained afterwards above four years in a state of licentiousness, all came into order in one day; and which goveroment they have steadily supported with their person and property ever since, now five years! A people, who not all the offers, threats, or intrigues of McGregor himself, nor those of his successors, Irvin, Hubbard, and Aury, nor the craft and influence of many others at Fernandina and elsewhere, could bring over one of them from their fidelity to the Spanish goyernment. A people, seven and twenty of whom sought for, gave battle to, and drove from the field above one hundred of McGregor's men, in a body, commanded by Irvin, in sight of their own quarters, without losing one drop of blood!

The representation I have handed in, as a record in their favour, is too long for insertion here; but a copy remains in my hands, and I trust will be read with general satisfaction. All papers laying in my possession, and appertaining to individuals of these districts, will be carefully distributed to their owners, as soon as leisure will permit me to attend to them.

Captain Bell has authorized, according to the proclamation of general Jackson, a continuance of all your offices and former functions, until laws are formed by higher authority for the government of the province. He recommends that the judiciary should be confined to such cases and matters as do not admit of, or require appeals beyond the exclusive jurisdiction of these magistrate courts ; that all others should lay over until farther orders. And he says, that all heinous invaders of the public peace will find safe keeping in the hands of the military at Fernandina if sent there.

Yours sincerely,

(Signed)   GEORGE I. F. CLARKE.

* * *

The proceedings of the United States in West Florida having been conducted by general Jackson, and repeatedly laid before the public, do not need repetition here. It would be an invidious task to detail the events that have occurred in East Florida since the exchange of flags. The variety of perplexing circumstances, the confluxion of laws, and the embarrassments arising from the great distance from the place whence orders emanated, which have successfully been the fate of St. Augustine, will, by the wisdom of congress, have entirely been removed, and forgotten before this book issues from the press. The only circumstance of much interest arose from the circumstance of the secretary of the province having a day or two after the cession, found it necessary in the absolute want of all law regulation, police, or magistracy, to exercise his authority upon the occurrence of some peculiar circumstances, respecting the carrying off of slaves, to confine for a very short time one of the citizens in the fort of Saint Augustine : five months afterwards, upon a trial before the county court, damages were awarded against captain Bell, when the inhabitants, by an unanimous resolution made up the fine by subscription, and the following letters were written to and from that gentleman, which having never been made generally known, are now laid before the public.

[TRANSLATION.]

John R. Bell, Esq. Captain of the United States Artillery.

St. Augustine, December 21, 1822.

Sir,

When a people receives from its rulers the protection due to the persons and property of the individuals who compose it, when such rulers cause the laws to be observed, and when their actions are guided by the general good, so that their fulfilment of their august charge, is consonant with the duties imposed on them by society, they make themselves at the same time, worthy of the esteem and gratitude of that community over whom they have presided.

The Floridians call to mind with pleasure the short but satisfactory period, when in you sir were united the civil and military command of this province, wherein we are aware you acted as far as was practicable for the public welfare, in the administration of justice; and consequently it was not with an ear of indifference that the sentence given by the court of this county was heard, amercing you in the sum of three hundred and seventeen dollars and four reals, for a proceeding, in which your sense of equity could not allow you to act otherwise than you did. It is not to be understood however, that the award of the court is called arbitrary or unjust; the people are too well aware of the respect due to all tribunals to attempt to trench upon their prerogatives : but they however know, that under the circumstances in which you gave the order, in consequence of which this fine has been laid, such a measure was necessary for the tranquillity of this place. In a country recently taken possession of by another government different in its laws, language and customs, wherein the new authorities have no definite knowledge of its inhabitants, its necessities, in a word of any thing, there must naturally result in the changes from one administration to the other some defects, which are consequences of the confusion reigning upon the establishment of a new system. What a vast field was there not opened for felons to commit in this state every species of crime ; and who is there that doubts the propriety of rigorous measures being adopted against them in the very outset ?

Under these views, the inhabitants and the proprietors of this city have been pleased to appoint us the subscribers to express to you their sentiments ; and we therefore, have the satisfaction of being their organs, for the purpose of offering the just tribute of gratitude to merit ; and they beg that you sir, will condescend to allow, that the damages be paid by them, we being authorised to deliver the amount immediately.

This is a general wish of the people, who can duly appreciate men, who, like yourself, have gained the esteem of many adherents, among whom are ranked,

Sir,

Your most obedient and affectionate servants.

[Signed]   GAB. G. PERPALL,

JOSEPH M. HERNANDEZ,

JOSIAH SMITH,

F. M. ARREDONDO,

BERNARDO SEGUI,

GUILLERMO TRAVERS.

St. Augustine, 22d December, 1821.

[ANSWER.]

Gentlemen,

I received your letter of this morning. The various emotions it has excited it is impossible for me to express. The language of feeling is brief ; and I must reply to it with the bluntness and since-rity of my profession.

I was called upon to exercise the undefined and dangerous powers entrusted to me by the governor of the Floridas. I would willingly have evaded this invidious trust, but I was commanded, and it was my duty to obey. I was not promised, have not expected, nor have I received any benefit for my services. I found myself called upon to protect a virtuous and industrious people, from the rapacity and violence of adventurers from every part of the world who looked for redemption from punishment, from the absence, as they supposed, of all law and government. I was actuated by a sincere desire of protecting the rights of the citizens of Florida, committed to my charge, without any regard to their being Spanish or American. I did not think it necessary to ascertain with legal precision, whether my powers were to be measured by the limits imposed by the old or new constitution of Spain. The good of all, the peace of the whole community were my only rule of conduct. I had no antipathies to indulge in, no resentments to satisfy. I was a stranger to all. If I have erred, if the verdict of a jury of my countrymen should at some future period, be brought up in array against me when circumstances are forgotten, I will powerfully appeal for my acquittal to your affectionate letter, and challenge the world to pronounce the person guilty of tyranny and oppression, who has received so unanimous a testimonial of approbation of his administration, from a people so feelingly alive to a sense of injustice, so warm hearted and so generous. I cannot therefore decline your offer.

The time is not far distant, when under the favoring influence of the American constitution, the virtues of the antient inhabitants and proprietors of Florida will be duly appreciated, when they will have to claim and will assert their right to the exercise of government, and when the base individuals, who now endeavour to set one portion of the community in array against the other, will receive due execration.

Be pleased to present my affectionate regard to the gentlemen whose sentiments of approbation you have conveyed, and for your-

selves, receive the gratitude for the feeling language in which it has
been expressed.

I remain your affectionate servant.

[Signed]   JNO. R. BELL.

To Messrs. Perpall, Hernandez, Smith, Arredondo, Segui and
  Travers.

On the part of the inhabitants and proprietors of the city of St. Au-
gustine.

Now that Florida is about to be governed by the wholesome laws
of a republic, and that the shackles which have hitherto impeded
her improvement are taken off, we may rationally look forward to
read in the page of her future annals prosperity, happiness and independence.   When the real superiority of our territory is duly
appreciated, it will be found pre-eminent in agricultural importance;
and when an extensive, industrious and respectable population send
their representatives to congress, Florida will be confessedly acknowledged not wanting in intellectual endowments ; and the present humble recorder of her resources looks forward to the time
when her future glory will be transmitted to after times, by the elegant pens of native historians.

TOPOGRAPHICAL OBSERVATIONS.

―――――――

The river Saint Mary, which is part of the northern boundary of Florida, was formerly supposed to have originated in the Oke-fin-o-cau swamp ; but this appears to be an error, as there is a high pine ridge between the source of the stream and the swamp. This circumstance was communicated to the author several years since by major-general Gaines, who had himself ascertained the fact. The upper branches of this river partake very much of the character of those of the Edisto and Combahee rivers, in South Carolina. There are a few saw mills erected there, and more probably might be built with advantage ; lower down the lands may be made capable of the cultivation of rice. The bar of Saint Mary's river has from 20 to 28 feet water. There are two entrances bold and safe ; the light-house is on the northern side of the entrance on Cumberland island ; Amelia island at the mouth of St. Mary's river, is well settled ; considerable quantities of fine live oak have been obtained from this island at various periods, but it is now almost gone, at least all the timber fit for large vessels of war. At the north end of Amelia island is the small town of Fernandina, which sprung up during the embargo in 1808, and the subsequent war. At present it droops ;

but the excellence of the anchorage opposite the place, will doubtless in due time make it more resorted to, and the town will again
flourish.

An inland navigation exists through the narrows between Amelia island and the main land. After passing the straits, Nassau
river discharges itself between Amelia and Talbot islands. This
river is supplied by many branches, and is navigable a considerable
distance up ; the lands are rich, but subject to inundations. Rice
plantations may certainly be established here, and made profitable.
Talbot and Fort George islands are seperated from the main by navigable creeks, and are fine cotton islands. These passed, the
mouth of the river St. John presents itself. Passing it by for the
present, we may proceed up Pablo creek, immediately opposite the
mouth of the branch separating Fort George island from the main.
The lands in the vicinity of Pablo are excellent, and in cultivation.
The sugar has been successfully tried for two years back by Major
Chairs. Pablo creek heads in Diego plains, as does also the North
river, which leads down to the harbor of Saint Augustine. A short
canal of a few miles in length would complete the inland navigation
from hence to Charleston. There is no inlet between the entrance
to Saint John's river, and Saint Augustine. The latter harbour is
good, but only affording 12 or 13 feet water, is very detrimental to
its increase as a commercial town. Leaving a description of the
town for another place, we shall at present follow the outline of the
coast.

The navigation from the harbour of St. Augustine to the bar of
Matanzas, along what is termed Matanzas river, though intricate, affords water for such vessels as can pass the latter entrance. The
St. Sebastian river, which forms the southern and western boundaries of the city, is of some width at its junction with Matanzas river ;
but owes its size chiefly to the influence of tide water : the head of
navigation, including all the windings of the stream, is scarcely ten

miles from its mouth, and merely serves to bring a little fire wood
into the town : It heads in two or three prongs, one of which, called
the Red-house branch, is a narrow but deep and rapid creek, affording scites for saw-mills, to be erected at some future time : Moultrie
creek has its mouth covered with several islands, and a long reef of
oyster banks and mud flats extend for some distance, forming a series of shoals, at which the tides from the respective inlets of St.
Augustine and Matanzas meet : Moses's creek fall into the river a
few miles north of the latter bar, joining it where the marsh on the
main side is wide and intersected by a labyrinth of small channels,
mostly dry at low water.   Matanzas river in its whole extent is only
separated from the Atlantic by Anastatia or Fish's island, which, at
the southern extremity, is very narrow, being little more than a sand
bank : upon a small island formed by the Matanzas' entrance on the
south, and a creek navigable for boats on the north, and terminating
Anastatia island, stands the old tower of Matanzas : the marshes here
are wide, but the water course very narrow, particularly in proceeding towards what was called the little bar ; the only access to
which, and to the creeks southwardly, is through an artificial vent
or canal, dug by the Spanish soldiers and Havana negroes by permission of the late government, a voluntary subscription having been
raised by three or four planters to pay them : on the site of this
was some short time back a natural creek, but a violent gale, completing the gradual accumulation of sand at the mouth of the little
bar (barra chica), filled that entrance at last and stopped the passage
of the waters towards the great Bar also : although the canal affords
a boat communication, yet it is insufficient to carry off the great body
of fresh water coming down from two large swamps, and the marshes on each side are completely overflown at present, more particularly on account of the heavy rains during the preceding season :
The water in its efforts to escape has already traced a channel towards the narrow sand bank which rises from the beach, and it is pro-

bable that in a few years the Barra Chica will be again opened near
the outlet.   The planters have also resolved to dig across the beach
and complete the opening of the inlet, the fresh waters having destroyed their oyster banks and prevented the sea fish from coming up.   Passing the narrows the course of the creek or channel
meanders through the extensive marshes to the junction of Hernandez's and Pellicer's creeks, about six or seven miles from the bar
of Matanzas and two miles less from the Barra Chica.   The former
stream twelve miles further south heads in Graham's swamp : the
latter is navigable some miles beyond Pellicer's house to where the
King's road formerly crossed it on a bridge, long since destroyed, and
heads far back in the pine lands : in Sawmill swamp, three or four
miles from Pellicer's point it receives a large addition from the drain
of Cawcaw swamp, wherein Moses's creek lately mentioned also
takes its rise.   The character of almost all the land between St.
Augustine and Pellicer's is indifferent : narrow skirts of hammock
fringe the borders of the creeks, and every spot of good land is covered by some title or other, many tracts having been successively
owned and abandoned by the unlucky and ignorant attempters at cultivation.   The plantations of Mr. Hernandez, Mr. Perpall, and
Mr. Pellicer are good, and the marsh and savanna lands in their vicinity when banked and drained would produce fine crops of sugar if
their vicinity to St. Augustine should tempt any one to undertake the
great labour.   The grounds planted by Mr. Hernandez, are
the northern point of a long narrow hammock called Graham's
swamp, extending as far as the Tomoca ferry (about thirty miles :)
its average breadth is scarcely three fourths of a mile.   Colonel Bulow, a rich planter of South Carolina has made extensive purchases
upon this swamp, and is preparing with a large force to establish
considerable sugar plantations.   On its east side scrub lands and
saw palmettos extend to the Atlantic : On its west immense
tracts of pine land spread to the river St. John : parallel and

at a short distance therefrom runs the main road southwardly
which is in general good, and has been lately cleared out and made
passable for a waggon, being one of the only three roads in the province which affords practicable travelling for any mode of conveyance
but horses : Eight miles beyond Pellicer's creek is a considerable
run of water, with the remains of a stupenduous mill-dam, constructed formerly by a Mr. Bernardino Sanchez : approaching Tomoca
one or two other creeks intervene, being the head waters of Smith's
and Ormond's creeks.   All the good land with one or two exceptions has already been taken up.   Upon Tomoca river was formerly an old ferry and the road to the town of New Smyrna proceeded on:
it is now quite grown up.   Haul-over creek and Tomoca river form
the head of Halifax river or Mosquito north lagoon : The junction
of the two latter forms an acute promotory called Mount Oswald :
Haul-over creek proceeeds northerly, its western branch or Smith's
creek heads in Graham's awamp, near which it receives Ormond's
creek, and another tributary water : the eastern branch skirts the
sea and near its head is scarce a furlong from it across which boats
are hauled by the fishermen : this haul-over is only fifteen miles from
the bar of Matanzas.

From Mount Oswald, Halifax river runs straight for upwards of
sixteen miles two points to the eastward of south : its average
breadth is about three quarters of a mile as far as Snake island and
Orange grove : here a low marshy projection denominated the isl-
and encroaches from the main upon the uniformity of the river's
width reducing it to less than half a mile at this northern point of a
bay ; within which is a stone house, being the last permanent inhabited building on the coast between St. Augustine and cape Florida :
it is occupied by a poor couple who seem to live in much poverty :
Mr. Anderson an enterprising planter from South Carolina has 40 or
50 hands employed in raising cotton at the Orange Grove plantation.
four miles south of this are the Pelican islands, from whence the river loses its open character, and winds among an innumerable clus-

ter of mangrove islands down to the bar of Mosquito, hugging the Atlantic shore : next the main are a variety of intricate passages connecting with each other and indenting the land : three separate
creeks penetrate the interior a little way, all being in some
measure connected with Spruce creek : some considerable quantity
of good land lies scattered about these waters, but too low for cultivation without much labour. The whole of the land fit for
agriculture, from Tomoca to Spruce creek, has been granted away :
the main body of it consists in a hammock which appears to be a
continuation of Graham's swamp, running parallel to Halifax river
a mile or two back, and one or two eligible tracts on the river above
the Pelican islands : the narrow skirt of land between the river and
the ocean is totally useless.

Mosquito or New Smyrna entrance is narrow, but affords water
for vessels drawing ten feet : the anchorage is good inside and on
the south shore a vessel may lay alongside and make fast to the mangroves within a mile of the bar. The scite of the abandoned town
of New Smyrna is five miles from the inlet, but presents no bluff or
elevation on the river, and is shut out from the sea breeze by the
cluster of mangrove islands in front. These islands are thickly
spread between the narrow beach and the main land over a space
from two to five miles in width : one channel on the west keeps
next the main : the eastern one after a very crooked course conducts
to Turtle Mount or Mount Tucker, the summit of which is about 80
feet above the level of Hillsborough river, as the channel is called.
It is a vast collection of shells chiefly oysters which appear to be the
work of Indians of other days.   Three miles further south is a beautiful body of hammock land called the Cigeras, which is perhaps unequalled by any in Florida : there appears to be about one thousand
acres in a body.   A few miles further south conduct to the entrance
of Mos quito south lagoon, where the western passage also enters.
This piece of water appears to average eight or ten miles in width,

and nearly thirty in length : with the exception of a few scattering
mangrove islands on the Atlantic side it is quite open : half way down
on the western side it is separated from Indian river by a narrow
isthmus which is only 1980 feet wide, called the Haulover, across
which canoes and boats are continually hauled. A canal could be
made here at an expense not exceeding one thousand dollars, which
would thereby complete a good inland navigation for upwards of
two hundred miles. Nearly all the good lands between this place
and Spruce creek northerly have been granted away, but the location of them is not so certain : from the nature of the ground the
tracts lie in two parallel lines ; the front on Hillsborough river and
Mosquito Lagoon forming one range, and Turnbull's back swamp
the other : this latter is situated back a few miles, extending from
Spruce creek and gradually shaping its course to the head of Indian
river. The main stream of the last water has one of its sources in
this swamp ; the other one called the North-west branch comes
from the N. N. W. and has a large body of good land about it, upon
which claims by grants exist, but the location is very doubtful.
There appears but little doubt that the head of this N. W. branch
of Indian river and the head lake of St. John's river, approach each
other very near heading in the same savanna or marsh : there has
always been a tradition of an existing communication between
these two, which an inspection of the map will explain. From the
union of this branch with the main river along the western shore, as
far down as eight miles below the Haulover the land is rich, but
encumbered with grants of some kind, many of which however there
is reason to believe are unlocated.

Indian river is a beautiful sheet of water : at the Haulover, it is
three or four miles wide, and so continues a long distance northward : in a southern direction it expands on the eastern side, and a
collection of mangrove islands skirt the shores as far as cape Canaveral. Fifteen miles from the Haulover is the north end of Meritt's

island, which stands in the centre of the Lagoon parallel to the shores,
with a broad stream each side. For more than forty miles it divides
the river, which averages three miles in breadth. On the main or
western side is the proper channel : the eastern branch is shallow
and its upper end spread¢ with flats and mangrove islands, confusing
the navigator and impeding the passage of all but small canoes. The
average extent across Meritt's island is two miles at least, which
gives upwards of 50,000 acres ; this is said to have been granted to
Mr. McIntosh of Georgia, and now belongs to Colonel Clinch of the
United States army. The quality of the land on the main is various
but in general good and improving as progress is made towards the
south ; the shores beginning to present an elevated appearance :
bluffs of shell rock rear themselves close on the river ; the flatness
visible over all the preceding country begins to disappear : the
foundation is rock under vegetable mould ; upon the surface is
shell stone ; limestone and slate is found in detached spots, and all
the geological signs indicate an approach to a higher and more
healthy region. Indeed after arriving at Meritt's island, there can
be but little doubt that the country is upon the river free from
those causes which produce bilious and intermittent complaints.
The grants here are less close to each other : the principal one is
to a Mr. Delespine, which was regularly made previous to the period stipulated in the treaty in return for supplies furnished the garrison at various periods : it has been regularly located and the
lines distinctly marked out by blazed trees. It is upon the back of
this and the adjoining tracts that was discovered an immense savanna through which the waters supplying the source of the river St.
John apparently flow. At a perpendicular distance of something
less than three miles from the bank of Indian river, its eastern side
is struck, and it presents a breadth of at least twelve miles. From
the top of the high pine trees on the margin, the course of waters
may be traced apparently a few miles distant, nearest the west

boundaries of the great prairie, beyond which the pine woods raise their heads. On Indian river some of the best hammocks in the Floridas are to be met with, healthy and elevated : the occasioned breaks of pine bluffs are rather advantageous than otherwise as presenting better scites for settlements. During the last twenty miles of the extent of Meritt's island, the west branch of Indian river is not more than from one and a half to two miles wide, being at the northern end six or seven : immediately opposite the south of the island which is a narrow point of rock and mangroves, is St. Antonio river or Elbow creek : a low rocky shore on each side ornamented with tufts of hammocks and a large entrance cove give it an handsome appearance : but immediately behind the hammock and pine lands, the stream is only to be navigated back two or three miles when it heads in a swamp, beyond which is a savanna.

The south entrance to the east channel of Indian river is scarcely 400 yards wide ; the banks a mile up however recede towards the beach, and it afterwards becomes near three miles across, to within ten miles of cape Canaveral, where it is but a trifling distance over the beach to the sea. Somewhat beyond, a promontory divides the water into two prongs ; the westward continues on till the channel is lost in the archipelago of mangrove keys at the north end of Meritt's island ; the other comes immediately behind the cape, between which and the south side of the Mosquito lagoon is a large lake of fresh water. The navigation on this east side of the island is extremely confused, and many shipwrecked persons attempting with their crafts to find an inland passage have lost their course, and being compelled to abandon their boats, have endeavored to travel along the beach, upon which they have been known to expire in the agonies of thirst, while the pond just alluded to was near them, and when a hole scratched on the sands but a few inches above the reach of the waves would have produced them excellent fresh water ; which may be also thus procured along every part of the Florida coast, both on the sea beach and the Lagoon banks; but in many unfortunate cases it has been unknown.

Two miles south of St. Antonio river is Crane creek, of which none of the persons who have previously navigated Indian river were aware; its mouth is almost covered by a point of land, lapping over, leaving a small narrow entrance on the south, not twenty yards across. Crane creek for half a mile up is wide, but it is soon confined in a narrow run, through a strip of marsh bordered by pine lands and heading in a piece of swamp; the sloping banks however in general are high, with fine tall pitch pine trees at large distances, the undergrowth grass with scattering shrubs, presenting in sailing up a handsome appearance resembling a European park. Game of all kinds is abundant, and as in all the other waters there appears great plenty of fish. This remark upon the pine lands here is applicable to many spots.

Two miles south St. Andre's river or Turkey creek empties into the lagoon; its right bank is altogether pine; on the left for a very short way some hammock scrub and spruce is to be found; it is but a small distance up that it separates into two springs, soon terminating in little swamps, having passed through high pine land.

Immediately beyond the mouth of this creek are the Turkey bluffs, of rich yellow sand and forty feet in height, extending a mile in length; this terminates the general low rocky shore which was predominant from within about twenty miles of the Haulover; a trifling distance further on the bluff is of shells with a scrub hammock, the northern sand bluff being covered with pines, and having a luxuriant under brush of oak and hickory scrub. The Turkey bluffs present one of the most healthy and beautiful spots to be met with on the eastern coast of Florida for houses; they are supposed to be the same as the hills marked in most of the charts, " *Las Tortolas.*" Pelican island is a small mangrove key eight miles south of Turkey creek, nearest the west shore; the beach from Meritt's island is bare of tall growth with only one tuft of tall pines, and one of cabbage trees, and no mangrove trees or bushes until thus far when they recommence. Five miles below is the mouth of St. Sebastian river, distant altogether eighteen miles from the south end of Meritt's island, and distinguished by a high red sand bluff on the south point of entrance. This stream like the three preceding ones has pine lands alone on its banks, which are in general very high bluffs of light colored sand. It comes from the S. S. E. in a very serpentine course, having its head among the flats, savannas, and ponds which lie parallel to the Indian river narrows, there extending southwardly.

The whole western shore from some miles north of Elbow creek, past St Sebastian river, and down to the vicinity of the narrows which are eleven miles beyond St. Sebastian, is in general pine land, but elevated and healthy with the opposite beach free from mangrove bushes, and therefore receiving the full action of the breeze from the sea, the shore of which is in general four miles distant, three of which are occupied by the breadth of Indian river.

Passing the narrows which are three miles through, and something more than a quarter wide, the pine lands recede from the west front of the Lagoon which is covered by fine marshes half a mile wide, beyond which is a low hammock of rich growth, and the character is retained as far as opposite to the bar of the river, a distance of thirteen miles : upon the beach side near the narrows are occasional pieces of good hammock, but the east bank of the river thence is fringed with mangroves and a line of islands of the same to the outlet, which is approached through a narrow channel two miles through among thick mangrove keys. The marshes are covered with the plant called pursley, and contain almost a solid body of clay : they are several feet above the surface of the water. The whole of this pine extent may contain about eight thousand acres, being one of the largest bodies of good soil to be met with. Fine hammocks with in general elevated scites, are found along from Indian river bar to the mouth of St. Lucie river ; but like all the others observed on or near the water courses of East Florida, their breadth seems limited to half a mile. The bay is several miles wide in this extent, with occasionally on the beach patches of good hammock land, among some of which are to be traced old fields and other indications of former settlements : the Gap sixteen miles from the bar is remarkable, giving at sea the appearance of an inlet : on the sea shore are the rocks of St. Lucie directly fronting the mouth of that river, indicating its position, and chiefly to be noted from the adjoining strand being called the money bank : a vessel with dollars having been lost here, coin has occasionally been found on the beach, and the tradition has sent many to search this mine, which however like many similar expeditions seems only to end in disappointment.

The majestic appearance of St. Lucie river affords at first sight the greatest expectations : disembogueing, by a mouth nearly a mile in width, its volume of waters into a wide and extensive bay, it gives the idea of its having traversed a long region from the west, perhaps originating in the much talked of lake Mayaco, which like the fountain of youth has never yet been found. The view of the first few miles of ascent is imposing ; on the north, a high rocky hill binding a rich vegetable soil, extending some distance back from the shore and six or seven miles along it ; a fine hammock growth of heavy timber presenting a beautiful appearance ; on the opposite side the bank is equally high, but covered with pine growth mixed with oak and hickory scrub ; between them a river whose breadth admitting a free circulation of sea air, at once convinces the traveller that on such a place health must reside.

At the forks ten miles from the mouth, the perspective is remarkably striking ; from the points of land three large sheets of water spread towards different points, and though pine is the prevalent growth of the river banks, yet it is of a good quality and affords a variety of places

where fruit culture would succeed; a fact which may no doubt hereafter populate this country with a race of industrious whites whom the
healthiness of the spot may allure hither. The south branch of St.
Lucie extends only about four miles when it stops suddenly and a
narrow creek covered with a green mantle of water plants alone remains, heading in a small swamp ; the northern branch may continue
ten or twelve miles in a N.W. direction, when it also suddenly, contracts in a similar manner and heads in a swamp beyond which savannas and ponds run parallel to the sea shore towards the head of
St. Sebastian river. The banks every where except the large hammocks at the mouth are covered with pines : two or three miles S.
W. of the forks is a body of hammock, and pine lands beyond that
again to the borders of a flat savanna country.

Proceeding to trace the inland navigation southwardly, some miles
beyond St. Lucie river are found Jupiter narrows, connecting the
sound or bay of Indian river with that of Jupiter or Hobe ; they
are eight or ten miles in length, with several narrow channels
through a body of mangrove islands lying between the sea beach and
the main land, on which latter are to be found small pieces of low
hammock well adapted for sugar.

The western shore of Jupiter sound presents a series of very high sand hills with undulating tops covered with forests of low
spruce pines ; one swell of high ground rising above the rest is called on marine charts the Bleach-yard, from the large spots of land un-
covered by vegetation, presenting to the coasting mariner the appearance of linen spread out on the hills upon the side next the beach;
a beautiful piece of land reaches from the mouth of the narrows four
miles, with a low rocky bluff generally on the river ; it may contain
about 1000 acres of first rate hammock, a part of which was cultivated
many years since by an old Spaniard named Padre Torre, and more recently was planted by one Hutchinson, with cocoa nuts, limes, plan-
tains, bananas, oranges, &c. which are said by the pilots to be still in

good bearing, though the place has been many years quite abandoned and grown up in thick bush. From this hammock is four miles to Jupiter inlet which is now closed.

Three large rivers coming altogether through a pine country, discharge into Grenville sound immediately at the south end of Jupiter bay, but the large body of water has too sluggish a current to force open the inlet which is closed by the sand, though opened occasionally by accidental circumstances. The three streams are distinguished as Grenville river on the north, Middle river, and Jupiter creek on the south; the latter as well as Fresh-water creek near the bar, have some connexion with the fresh water lake which approaches within four miles of Jupiter, by means of lagoons and marshes, through which a channel might easily be dug; thereby with another short cut on the south, making a complete though intricate communication practicable at least for boats, from cape Florida and the keys to within forty miles of St. Augustine; as will appear by the subsequent parts of this report, and a reference to the map now publishing.

This lake is thirty-five or forty miles in length, with marshes at its south end, which contain a body of such fine sugar land, that it will not be long ere it is brought into cultivation, and the canal that is made to drain it will finish the only remaining part of the inland navigation, connecting the south end of fresh water lake with the north end of Rio Seco; which spot is indicated by an orange grove near the beach, to which from Jupiter inlet the *present* mode of access, is by hauling the boat or canoe across at both places, the intermediate distance of forty-five miles being run along the coast at sea.

The Rio Seco winds in a very serpentine course through a body of marsh at first, and latterly mangrove islands to its mouth, which is closed at present like that of Jupiter; the place where the outlet was is also called Boca Ratone and Dry inlet; patches of hammock are occasionally to be found on the main side, but the chief growth is pine ; a mile or two west in the woods is the large lake which gives rise to Jupiter creek.

Boca Ratone sound receives also from the south another creek, heading in large marsh flats, but with deep water ; the whole of which together with that from the Rio Seco, unable to discharge itself over the dry inlet, has forced itself by a natural canal through a neck of high land into the Middle river at the place where a stream called the Potomac runs into it ; the rush of the water through this narrow channel is very great, the current driving with a velocity capable of giving motion to the largest wheels, and upon it several saw-mills might work with advantage, should the Florida pitch pine which is abundantly supplied by the adjacent woods, ever become in sufficient demand as lumber. The Potomac river, as the few occasional visitors here have named it, is merely the head of Middle river, its course is through a pine country of good quality, heading in swamps and savannas, and connected with the *Great Glade* which will be described.

The outlet of Middle river is now better known as Hillsborough, and a precisely similar communication exists from hence to New river, as the north route to Boca Ratone. New river and all the branches discharging through its bar originate in the Great Glade, running through pine lands and heading in cypress swamps, which have previously been inundated from the Glade : the inland communication from New river to cape Florida, is from the head of New river to the head of the Rio Ratones through the Glade. On the former are some occasional spots of good land, with elevated pine lands, healthy and of good quality. The Ratones discharge into the head of the Bay of Key Biscayne, somewhat as delineated in the latest charts of the Florida coast, but no good land is to be found except immediately behind Cape Florida, where a small piece of hammock exists on the high rocky front generally, as upon Key Biscayne Bank : a little further south, strips of similar growth are occasionally to be

7

found, but beyond all are pine lands and mangroves, as far as the
vicinity of cape Sable, and even there but in very small quantities. *the hammocks are*
From cape Sable to cape Romano, the land is low with mangrove
bushes, closing the banks of small streams draining from the Great
Glade, with small pieces of hammock and long necks of pine land
intermixed. Forests of pine are known to extend on the coast from
cape Romano to Charlotte harbour, intermixed with excellent pieces of hammock, but beyond that it is not pretended to make any
statement in this report.

The Glade, or as it is emphatically termed the *Never Glade*, appears
to occupy almost the whole interior from about the parallel of Jupiter inlet to cape Florida, thence round to cape Sable to which
point it approaches very near, and northwardly as far as the Delaware river discharging into Charlotte bay : its general appearance
is a flat sandy surface mixed in the large stones and rocks, with from
six inches to two feet of water lying upon it, in which is a growth of
saw, and other water grasses, so thick as to impede the passage of
boats where there is no current. Over this are a number of islands
and promontories, many of which are altogether of hammock growth,
with mixtures of pine and cabbage tree land, each spot doubtless
capable in some degree of cultivation ; but deteriorated by being placed in a situation so difficult of access, and exhibiting so forbidding an
aspect, that for the present the attempts to penetrate across have
been repelled, and the dissatisfied traveller has been sent back unable to complete the object of his mission, and confused in his effort to
tread the mazes of this labyrinth of morasses. Towards its northern
end however it contracts considerably, and then changes somewhat
of its character by assuming the appearance of an open cypress
pond, which extends to the great swamp and savanna at the head of
the river St. John and Ocklawaha, and *here* is a passage across ; for
it is a well ascertained fact, corroborated particularly in the author's
last voyage undertaken on the Peninsula, that the crossing place of

the Indians is made in a direction west of Jupiter inlet, and in their travels from the nation, by crossing the Haffia or Manatee river, and journeying in a S. E. course along the edge of the savanna swamp or morass to the narrowest spot, the passage over which occupies three days continued travel in water.

The determination of the circumstance of this immense body of low land occupying the whole southern interior of East Florida, easily affords an explanation of those delineations upon antient maps, representing it as cut up by rivers and lagoons, communicating with each other and the sea ; and it is by no means improbable that the knowledge of its existence, prevented the late government from commencing settlements in a country of so little promise, for had the regions boasted of as equal to Cuba existed here, there is enough of speculation in that island, to have improved the land of promise long before this period.

On looking back over the preceding pages the reader must be struck with the reflection, that the sources from whence the various water courses of the Eastern coast of Florida originate, are not the pure springs of a hilly region, but a series of connected reservoirs, from whence exude in languid streams their vast collections of waters, a circumstance which under the almost tropical sun of this country might produce eternal diseases, had not the provident hand of nature raised a border of high lands nearly all around upon the sea coast of considerable breadth, and sent the never failing eastern wind to drive back the miasmæ to the interior : this belt appears to average five or six miles across including varieties of soil ; and while the future settlers upon the east coast of Florida, may be assured of no sickness assailing them from the marsh behind, they are protected from the encroachments of, and inconveniences attendant on a direct exposure to the ocean, by a narrow strip of land intervening between the sea and the long lagoons, that run in a parallel direction to the coast, on its whole extent nearly, affording an inland navigation almost uninterrupted and which cannot but soon be fully perfected.

The Florida reef and chain of keys commence at Key Biscayne or cape Florida. They are sufficiently interesting to be made the subject of a separate section, and therefore we go at once to cape Sable, the southern promontory on the side of the gulf of Mexico.

The advantages on this western side are not so equal, as in general from cape Sable to punta Largo, the land is low and covered with mangroves ; north of the latter promontory the belt around the central marsh is wider, and a succession of high pine lands with rich hammocks thickly intermixed, and a similar coast to that upon the Atlantic, make the extent as far as Tampa bay on a level with it in most points.

Immediately off cape Sable within musket shot of the shore, is a safe anchorage at all times in nine feet water. At Cape Sable or punta Tancha there are actually three capes, at the middle one of which are fresh water wells : these wells are distinguished by a tuft of button trees or white mangroves, being the only trees on the point.

The land at these capes and for some miles eastwardly is very good ; of a rich grey soil thickly mixed in with broken shells, presenting an even surface like a meadow, without a bush : this was called many years ago the Yamasee old field, but there appears every reason to suppose it a natural prairie. Behind this strip of land which is but narrow, rise hammocks of the usual width, a nd beyond a boundless savanna, the soil of which is richly alluvial and perfectly dry for a great distance ; but mingling at length with the Ever Glades. Among the numerous tropical productions in the hammocks are a few trees called *Huava*, of the palm family, from the leaves of which the fine straw Havana hats are made : some live oaks and vines of an amazing size. If coffee can be produced at all in Florida, this is the spot where it may be expected to succeed.

Cape Sable creek, immediately north of punta Tancha runs up in about an E. N. E. course through mangrove islands, marsh and clusters of hammocks, among the growth of which are cedar and small mahogany ; it spreads occasionally into lakes, and heads like all the other streams in the Eternal Glades.

The bight between cape Sable and punta Largo, or cape Romano, is called the bay of Juan Ponce de Leon, the upper or northern part being known as Chatham bay : here the Delaware or Gallivan's river discharges itself over a bar of eight feet water. This is a beautiful stream, and its high banks present most eligible scites for a town ; the lands on each side are represented as rich and luxuriant ; it heads in lake Macaco, or at all events in large lagoons in the recesses of the Ever Glade morass.

Immediately under cape Romano is anchorage for vessels of ten feet : from the cape to bay Carlos the coast is low, with forests of pine coming almost down to the edge of the sea. The river Coolasahatchie is the only stream of importance between these places.

Charlotte harbour has four inlets formed by a chain of islands ; upon the bar of the largest entrance is sixteen feet water. The bay within is spacious and sheltered ; it receives the waters of Charlotte river, a large and powerful stream with several large branches, and heading in lake Macaco. Although this lake is laid down on the map, yet its existence does not appear to have been actually ascertained by recent observations : so many former accounts however speak of it, giving it a location, that it has not been thought proper to omit it altogether, for there must be various collections of water in the Ever Glades, which to the eye of a hasty traveller might well appear as lakes and lagoons. Between Charlotte harbour and Tampa bay the land is double, that is, an inland navigation is afforded between the ocean and the main land by a chain of islands : this is not quite complete, but the coast partakes more of the character of the Atlantic seaboard than it has hitherto done.

Spirito Santo or Tampa bay is a spacious harbour, admitting vessels of twenty-four feet draught of water : it penetrates the coast in nearly an easterly direction, being some miles in width ; at its upper end it divides ; the north-western is called Tampa bay proper, the north-eastern takes the designation of Hillsborough bay. Tampa bay proper is only a shallow lagoon which receives no tributary waters ; two or three rivers discharge into Hillsborough bay. The various contradictory names given to them at different times, render it difficult to determine what are their respective true appellations. The lands upon Spirito Santo bay are low, but immediately back to the north-east they rise into beautiful undulations to the east and south-east. The plains of the Haffia are fertile, extensive and pleasing. There appears but little doubt that the savannas and low grounds at the head of this river extend to and connect with those, whence emanate the Ocklawaha and St. John's rivers, a circumstance that will be more apparent when the interior of the country is described.

From Tampa bay to the mouth of the Amisura river the coast is low, and the entrance to that stream is very shallow and extremely difficult to find : it is much to be lamented that so fine a water should have so shallow an outlet ; it forks a few miles up, the N. E. branch heading up the near skirts of what is known as the Alachua country ; the S. E. branches receive the waters from the large bodies of hammock and other rich land, lying near the present Indian towns, meandering through a beautiful region. A very wide and shallow bay extends from the mouth of the Amisura to that of the Suwanee : the coast is low and broken, and clusters of small keys are spread along. Several minor streams fall into the northern part of this large indentation, which receives the particular denomination of Vacasassy bay, from an antient Indian village in that vicinity.

The Suwanee, formerly called the San Juan, and corrupted by the Indian negroes to its present appellation, is a magnificent river ; by the quantity of mud and sand from the fresh water brought down, a large bar has been formed at the mouth, and the land appears like the Missisippi, by the alluvial depositions, to have encroached upon the sea. A low coast covered with cabbage trees intervenes to the entrance of the Chattahatchie or Saint Pedro river, which comes from the northward, heading about the Georgia lines, near the place where antient Spanish settlements once existed. Some miles further west the Ausilly, a handsome stream, falls into the bay of Appalachie ; its source is in the western parts of Georgia ; heavy inundations in the rainy seasons cover the banks of these waters for many miles, and render a circuitous route to fort St. Marks absolutely necessary.

The estuary at the head of the Bay of Appalachie receives two small rivers, at the junction of which is placed the small fortification of St. Marks : this post has never increased beyond a military position, to which the troops were generally confined : a trading house for the Indians has generally been established here. St. Mark's river heads some few miles to the N. E. at the Mickasukee towns, and the Wackhulla or Tagabona at the Talahassie hammocks near the scite of the old settlements of St. Louis. The Ocklockonne Bay receives the waters of the river of that name and of several smaller streams ; and there is an inland navigation to New river which is continued along St. George's sound to the mouth of the Appalachicola river, which is the true boundary of East and West Florida.

The lower parts of the rivers are subject to very deep and annual inundations, but the whole country from the Georgia line, many miles south from the bluff on the Appalachicola to the banks of the Suwanee is covered with fine rich hammocks, which have a great reputation for fertility. It is upon all the ungranted lands between these two latter rivers, that a project has been made, and probably will be executed for the purpose of concentrating all the Indians of both Floridas.

St. Joseph's bay and inlet is the first harbour in West Florida after doubling cape St. Blas ; it may be used as a shelter from hurricanes or violent gales with much advantage for small vessels, as may also St. Andrew's bay, which is a deep estuary with several arms receiving the waters of Ekanfinna river.

Santa Rosa inlet, thirty miles further to the westward, conducts to the bay of that name, which is of very great extent. The Choctawhatchie river, and all its tributary streams discharge into the eastern end of this bay ; and near the western end a number of small boggy creeks drain the vallies of the adjacent pine lands.

An inland navigation behind Santa Rosa Island conducts to the celebrated harbour of Pensacola, which spreading two large arms deep into the interior collects the Yellow water river, Middle river and its numerous branches ; the Escambia and its labyrinth of adjacent waters, and several smaller and less important streams.

Upon a dry healthy point of land and fronting the ocean is built the town of Pensacola, which only wants the hand of protection applied, and the spirit of enterprise diffused over it to cause its increase and prosperity : possessing a deep entrance and notwithstanding its recent severe affliction, having every assurance of health, it might become the depot for all those productions which are now placed at Mobile : a very small canal would unite the two bays, and thus open the channel for the tide of commerce : but this can only be expected by the union of both towns under the same state government.

Before proceeding to a description of the interior of the provinces, the author claims the privilege of introducing a few remarks on the political connexion between East and West Florida, which have arisen from a review of the attendant circumstances, and as it contains the concurrent opinions of many well wishers to both provinces, he offers it respectfully to the public.

West Florida has been gradually pared down to the present remnant : the large portions of country which have successively fallen to the share of Louisiana, Missisippi and Alabama have left bnt a narrow strip of land between the Perdido and Appalachicola rivers : and deprived of its original ports of New-Orleans and Mobile, West Florida must, like Poland, be distributed among the adjoining states : it will disappear from the map of America, by the ultimate annexation of Pensacola and the remaining portion of territory to Alabama, a step called for by reason and polity.

That such a course must be highly desirable for East Florida, will be readily acknowledged on a consideration of the subject : and it can easily be conceded, that it will not in anywise interfere with the national question of the entrance of another state into the Union.

From their more geographical juxta-position, East and West Florida have been perhaps considered by those at a distance as integrally united : that this is by no means the case is but too well known to their inhabitants ; for so dissimilar are their opinions, that even in this early stage of their independent existence, dissensions and discordance have sprung up, which a separate administration instead of conciliating appears rather to have tended to foster, and the dispute as to the seat of territorial government has already assumed a decided shape.

The eligible intended location of the Florida Indians between the Appalachicola and Suwanee rivers, will in addition to the present obstructed communication, place an Indian country between East and West Florida, and thus consummate the separation, which will then only want the fiat of Congress to render politically permanent.

The annexation of West Florida to Alabama will not add another representative in Congress to the latter commonwealth, nor will it prevent Florida from assuming its place in the Federal Union in due time, by abstracting so much population ; for it is towards East

Florida alone that the great mass of emigration will roll ; the warmer latitudes of the peninsula hold out anticipations of more lucrative
productions than West Florida : that country not extending beyond
the parallel already tried by our citizens, cannot present attractions
superior to the region between lake Borgne and Mobile, where is
found a soil at all events equal to any in West Florida.

Why should the Federal Government be burthened at present
with a double set of officers ?   Or why should the members of the
territorial legislature, be alternately condemned to emigrate as it
were to each extreme of the country.   At present while the population of West Florida is but few, it can be but a matter of indifference
to any but the residents of Pensacola, whether they obey the laws
of Alabama or Florida ; their rights are in either case equal ; and the
views of those who look for the aggrandizement of Pensacola, by the
diversion of the trade of the interior from the bay of Mobile to that
of the former place, can only be realized by an annexation to Alabama.   Pensacola can never be the seat of government ; and while
its citizens claim an imaginary honor, by seeking to keep it under its
antient rules, they prevent the very advantages they sigh for.

On casting a view over the map of the United States, the most un-
reflecting observer must be struck with the mere geographical propriety of the annexation ; a step that would relieve the general government of a contribution, accelerate the organization of West Florida, diminish the coming taxes, and take a dead weight from off the
remaining part of the territory.

As a matter of general interest to both provinces, it may be remarked that under the present organization, the governor cannot give
his attention to one section without detriment to the other, and where
the laws of Congress require certain oaths and formalities to be made
before him by the territorial officers, months may elapse and the
public interests suffer ere it can be done.

In thus hastily marking a few of the principle reasons for the annexation, the author deprecates the idea of being supposed to advocate the interests of East, at the expense of those of West Florida : he is perfectly convinced that it would be to their mutual advantage in every respect, and appeals to their own good sense to confirm that such is the case.

Having in the preceding pages briefly sketched an outline of the coast, we may proceed to examine the interior by counties, into which it has lately been divided by the legislative council of Florida.

Escambia County comprehends all that part of West Florida lying between the Perdido and Appalachicola *Choctaw* rivers, with Pensacola as the seat of justice. In the immediate neighbourhood of this city the character of the land is dry and sandy, its scite having been chosen for health. The good lands on the Coenecuh and Escambia rivers do not begin until their forks at Miller's, the lower parts being subject to be overflown ; the same holds good of the other waters discharging into the bay of Pensacola. Immense ridges of pine lands fill up the space from the banks of the Yellow Water to the Choctawhatchie, but on the head branches of both these rivers, near the northern line of the province, good lands are to be found, which will doubtless repay the labour of the industrious planter.

There are many Indian paths through this county, one particularly leading from near the mouths of the Choctawhatchie, all along the sea beach to the Signal tower at the entrance of Pensacola harbour : another traverses the pine ridges from the Coosada old town to the east point opposite the city of Pensacola : another leads from the same place, going round the heads of the branches of the Yellow-water, Middle and Coenecuh rivers. This latter river is navigable for small craft to the northward of the dividing line of the 31st degree of north latitude between Florida and Alabama, though the tide flows up but a few miles. The Choctawhatchie and its principal tributary branches are likewise navigable as far up as the Coosada old town nearly, and the produce will readily find its way to Pensacola, by way of Santa Rosa sound.

The former harbour abounds with fine scale and shell fish, but a vessel lying in its waters not coppered would be ruined in two months by the worms : craft obliged to remain there ought to be hove down, cleaned and payed once in five or six weeks.

It is more than probable that the northern parts of this and the adjacent counties of Jackson and Duval, are subject in the autumn to those bilious intermittent disorders known commonly at the south as the country fevers. So entirely *continental* is their situation that it cannot be expected they are different ; but the deep indentation of the salt waters of Pensacola and Santa Rosa bays, with the high sandy ridges in their vicinities, induce an expectation of health. The last summer has most unfortunately desolated the town of Pensacola, but this is the first time such a calamity has been known there, and without attempting to enter into the doctrine of importation or local generation of yellow fever, we may naturally infer that the origin of that fatal disorder was in this instance far from being local.

Respecting the culture most favourable for the soil of Escambia county, the trials in the neighbourhood of Mobile will best decide : it is certainly a fact that there is a greater degree of cold in this part of Florida than on the same parallel on the Atlantic coast, though not so much more as to prevent the cultivation of the sugar cane on favourable spots ; but it appears undoubted that the varieties of the grape may be introduced, and by a judicious culture be made much more profitable than can be expected from cotton, whose daily declining price forcibly tells us that the growth is far beyond the demand, and no alteration is apparently to take place for some time. It cannot however be disguised that fertility is by no means

the general characteristic of Escambia county, although many spots
are to be found equal to the most favoured situations in the southern
countries.

Jackson County comprehends the remainder of West Florida, to
which in order as it were to amalgamate the two provinces, a large
section from East Florida has been annexed, extending as far as the
Suwanee.

The characteristics of the seaboard of this county are similar to
those of Escambia, as far at least as cape St. Blas : the line of distinction between the upper and lower parts of the district thus far is
distinctly traced by a chain of hilly lands of a romantic character.
Over the Ekanfinna river is a natural bridge of rocks, a singularity
which distinguishes several parts of Florida.

North of the Weemico and in the forks between the Chamiooly
and Appilachicola rivers, are extensive tracts of fertile land : over
the Chamiooly is another natural bridge, and a series of small Indian
towns, one built on the right bank of the latter as far up almost as
the Alabama line ; this region is extremely well watered, but from
its geographical position must be subject to the annual endemics of
the adjacent territories.

The Appalachicola river has near its mouth, many channels to
discharge the vast volumes of water brought down ; upon these
islands rich crops of rice and sugar may doubtless be raised, as well
as upon the adjacent banks. The town of Colinton is laid off on
Prospect bluff, where fort Gadsden, better known as the Negro fort
once stood : it was here that a large body of refugee slaves took a
desperate stand, and were almost wholly annihilated by the blowing
up of their magazine when attacked by the troops of the United
States. This town will probably become a commercial place,
though the bar here having but twelve feet water, will prove as in
some other parts of Florida, a serious drawback.

The large region between the Appalachicola and St. Mark's rivers, bounded northwardly by the old Indian path from the Spanish bluffs to that fort, is the purchase made by the house of Panton, Leslie and Co. which is now known under the firm of John Forbes & Co. of Matanzas in the island of Cuba; it is commonly called Forbes's purchase, having been bought by that house from the Indians under the sanction of the Spanish government, for vast debts due by the various Indians at the respective trading houses of the firm in Florida, of which they had an exclusive monopoly ; the northern parts of this purchase are very fine lands, which character extends to the Georgia boundary.   There are of course large tracts of pine, but these are by no means of the worst quality.   A variety of rich grounds stretch in a N. E. direction from this tract to the Mikasukie towns, and at the banks of the Ocklockonne commence that series of old settlements, which extend along the main path to St. John's river. The traditions concerning these places are that they were peopled by small colonies of Spaniards, but when, is lost in the lapse of *time* ; yet the numerous Spanish names which still exist, though corrupted, seem to corroborate the assertion.   The period of this colonization must have been some time in the seventeenth century : Romans states that there was in his time a church bell lying in the old fields near the Santafe, or as it is now called the Santaffy river.

Two principal paths lead through Jackson county ; one running parallel with the sea coast from the White Kings town on the Suwanee to fort St. Marks, often impassable by inundations ; thence traversing Forbes's purchase, crossing the Appalachicola at the Spanish bluffs, and after traversing the Ekanfinna over the natural bridge, proceeds to the head of Santa Rosa bay.   The other road leaves the Suawanee many miles higher up, and passing through Mikasukie and by fort Scott on the frontiers of Georgia, crosses Chattahootchie and Flint rivers above their junction. Here the road branches, one passing the Chipola over a natural bridge, and joining the southern road near the head of St. Andrew's bay ; the other continues nearly parallel to the Alabama line to the Coosada old town. In communicating between Pensacola and St. Augustine neither of these roads are used, as the fords and ferries are scarcely ever practicable, and there are no accommodations, and scarcely inhabitants. The journey is performed by a circuitous route through Georgia and Alabama; nor is this great inconvenience likely to be soon remedied, as the travelling will be long too limited to induce persons to establish regular places of rest along so solitary a route ; and even should the Indians not be concentrated here as has been proposed, several years must elapse before United States' sales can be effected, and population come in ; and except Forbes's purchase, it is believed that no concessions have been made in this section.

The Suwanee river divides Jackson and Duval counties, and as well as some of its chief tributary waters take rise in Georgia. The Outhlacuchy has long ramifications and comes from the N. W.

The Alapapaha to which name the title Suwanee gives place above its junction with the Little Suwanee, has two equal branches which come from the north, after watering a large extent of land in Georgia. The little Suwanee or little St. John's river heads in the celebrated Oke-fin-o-cau swamp, and is almost the only drain that large tract of low land has. The recent surveys of the new counties of Georgia have demonstrated the size of the Oke-fin-o-cau to be very much less than was originally supposed : some of the earlier maps have represented it as occupying half the distance to the Flint and Chattahootchie rivers.

Too little is known of the general interior of Jackson county to give such minute topographical detail as is desirable, and unable to speak decidedly on many points, the author has judged it more advisable to be silent, than to swell his pages with mere speculative observations on an unexplored territory.

Duval county lies north of a line, drawn from the Cowford upon St. John's river to the mouth of Suwanee, and is naturally subdivi—

ded into two districts of different sizes , which Brandy creek falling
into the St. Mary's, seems to separate the western subdivision ₰ between the Georgia boundary and the head branches of the north
arm of the Santaffy river, are pine lands which are mostly low : on
the left bank of the Suwanee, and on New river, as well as the little
St. John's, fertile lands are to be met with : but the general appearance is unprepossessing, although in the centre a ridge of more elevated country spreads along, dividing the waters that flow into the
opposite seas.　But around the Santaffy and all its streams, an undulating pleasing landscape and rich productive lands commence, giving
indications of a material change being about to be observed, and we
enter a region which will be more minutely described presently.

We pause an instant here to mention the singular circumstances
of the Santaffy river, some considerable distance from its junction
with the Suwanee, sinking into the earth and rising again at a distance
of three miles : this space is called the Natural bridge, and here an
Indian path crosses : it is stated that in times of high freshets, the
space above the subterraneous channel is inundated, and that on those
occasions a parallel current runs over it : Weechatomoka creek,
a branch of the Santaffy. has a similar singularity, sinking precisely
in the same manner for half a mile.　A few miles below the White
Kings old town on the Suwanee, upon the left bank, is the spring
mentioned by the younger Bartram in his travels, wherein the manatee or sea-cow is often seen and sometimes caught.

The eastern or maritime district of Duval county contains Nassau
river and its numerous prongs, and little St. Mary's river : the lands
upon all these waters are in general very fine and peculiarly well
adapted for the cultivation of sea-island cotton.　A large body of
population are concentrated here, which was the northern district of
East Florida alluded to in a former part of these observations.

Deep marshes fringe the lower part of St. Mary's and Nassau
rivers, and the connecting inland navigation. A large road, formerly

kept in excellent repair leads from the Cowford on St. John's river, to Coleraine and camp Pinckney on the St. Mary's : it is part of what was once called the King's road, and is the only direct outlet by land from St. Augustine. After passing the head swamps of Nassau river, a path leads down to Waterman's bluff, on Belle river, nearly opposite the town of St. Mary's : near Coleraine another path diverges southwardly leading to the Alachua country, and an old trail exists from the Cowford ferry, crossing the high hills that divide the waters of Black creek from those of St. Mary's river, and leading round the head branches of the Santaffy to Suwanee river.

It is along the King's road that the mail should come to St. Augustine : Jefferson in Georgia being made the distributing post office, instead of St. Mary's; whence at present it is sent by water as far as Pablo creek at the mouth of the St. John's river ; much time, distance and inconvenience would be saved by this arrangement, and a semi-weekly instead of a weekly post, be established to the capital of East Florida.

Probably Duval county will receive the first impressions of an influx of population, which must speedily be spread over the country : it presents many attractions, and its vicinity to Georgia may induce the inhabitants of that state, who are already very favorably impressed with Florida, to make it their abode. Not many grants are in the western district, though probably the maritime portion is nearly all covered with larger or smaller concessions.

Saint John's county includes the remainder of the peninsula of East Florida, south of the line drawn from the Cowford ferry, on St. John's river, to the mouth of the Suwanee. It is from this division of the new territory, that greater expectations are formed on account of its extending into tropical regions : in order to treat of it more systematically, it will be adviseable to distribute the country into certain subdivisions : making all to the eastward of St. John's river the subject of one, and all to the westward of another ; the twenty-eighth

9

degree of latitude being the southern line of these two : and again below that parallel, considering the chain of low lands as a division between the Atlantic and Mexican districts of the rest of Florida.

The first of these subdivisions is the extent upon which almost all the previous effortsof its European possessors were lavished, to bring it forward in civilization and agricultural improvement : within this narrow neck of land, with the exception of the maritime part of Duval county, all the white population of East Florida has been concentrated, and in the Spanish regime absolutely confined, for few if any ventured to cross the river St. John above Black creek, deterred by the hostile attitude of the Indians.

The general characteristic of this portion of Florida is flat, and unprepossessing : but there are upon it many fertile tracts which will, when the hand of industry is judicially applied yield profitable returns.   It is remarkable that this part of the new country, which had once made large advances in the path of civilization, should have so retrograted and have become in many parts as great a wilderness as in its primitive state : the withering influence of the *old* system of Spanish government perhaps occasioned this, by hitherto casting its blight around, and for forty years impeding the natural advantages of the country from being improved, by those willing and capable of the task.

In all the accounts which have appeared respecting the peninsula of East Florida, it has been a customary and primary remark that the river St. John was the most prominent feature ; the observation must be reiterated ; that majestic flow of water occupying so remarkable a place on the map, the appearance of the channel of its course being so varied, and the magnificent growth of timber clothing its banks, gives it at once to the eye of a traveller the importance assigned to it by all writers.   Hitherto its source has been considered as undetermined ; but the late exploring and surveying expedition of captain Le Conte of the United States' Topographical Engineers has set that question at rest : indeed the elder Bartram fifty years since, pursued the same route and arrived at the identical head lake, which terminated captain Le Conte's expedition.

Tracing it back from its mouth, we find that lying in latitude 30° 18′ N. with twelve feet water on the bar at ordinary tides : the distance between the nearest points of land is about one mile ; the first remarkable place after passing the mouth of Pablo creek is Kingsley's bluff, six or seven miles from the entrance on the right bank ; it is about twenty-five feet high, with a table land of some extent, presenting an eligible scite for a town, which it is the intention of the proprietor to lay out. The ship-yard on the same bluff, is well adapted for the purposes which its name indicates.

The Cowford or pass St. Nicholas, twenty eight miles from the bar, is distinguished by its narrowness, being scarcely one thousand yards across, contrasting with the other reaches of the stream which are very wide. The high road laid out by the British and kept up by them and still called the King's road, crosses here.

The line of the river which thus far has been perpendicular to the trend of the sea coast, here suddenly forms a right angle becoming parallel thereto, and for the next thirty or forty miles dilates into a succession of lakes or deep bays, never less than three and sometimes exceeding six miles in breadth. At one of the widest parts, a few miles above the Cowford, is the mouth of Black creek, navigable fifteen miles for large vessels to the forks. A few miles above the mouth of Black creek stands the old block house of Picolati : nothing remains of it except two of the shattered walls, through which loop holes and *meutrieres* are pierced : it stands on a low bluff and half concealed by the luxuriant branches of surrounding trees, it reminds the visitor who views it from the river, of the deserted castellated residence of some antient feudal lord. On the opposite or west side of the St. John's was fort Poppa, of which scarce a vestage remains.

At the old Buena Vista station the river begins to wind in reaches, its general direction being still parallel to the ocean. The Alachua ferry is only one mile across. The stream after passing the Devil's Elbow widens again, and receives by several mouths the waters of Dunn's lake : passing Buffalo bluff, a beautiful and fertile spot, its character is slightly varied by a chain of swamp islands, of which Bartram makes mention and accurately describes in the third chapter of his travels : At the mouth of the Ocklawaha, the river expands into a little lake and continues in that character to lake George whose entrance is covered by Drayton's island. After crossing this beautiful piece of water, which is about eighteen miles in length and eight or nine in breadth, the St. John's may be rightly designated as a river.

The western banks of lake George are almost wholly pine : two beautiful streams called the Salt and Silver springs empty on this side : behind the pine ridges, extensive tracts of scrub land occupy almost the whole neck between lake George and the Ocklawaha river, extending southwardly in long prongs for many miles. The eastern banks have several orange groves, but the hammocks are not deep ; indeed the isthmus between lake George and Dunn's lake is chiefly pine lands.

A bar at the southward of lake George, prevents the passage of vessels drawing more than five feet water, up the river : a few miles beyond is the *Volusia* settlement, on the east side of the St. John's, a flourishing and well settled plantation, where the sugar cane has this last year been raised with the most flattering prospects, having ripened nearly six feet by the middle of November. *Hope hill* establishment, a little higher up, is also a good tract of land, and settling with much enterprise.

Spring-garden branch comes through a tract of rich land, and augments the volume of the St. John's, which here begins to wind and pursue a tortuous course, driving almost in a S. E. direction : Alexander's creek comes in near a small lake, on the banks of which is an old settlement called Beresford's cowpen : beyond this the stream grows narrow, and at length heads in a lake of about ten miles in perimeter, beyond which there is no visible progress. The latitude of this place is about 28° 40' N. according to captain Le Conte's observations.

From Alexander's creek upwards the St. John's meanders through extensive fresh marshes, dotted with islets of orange and live oak growth. At the head lake the water is several feet deep, and flows through the thick saw grass, flags and rushes, with some considerable current ; and as far as the eye can reach the marsh or savanna appears to be interminable : its extent cannot be accurately defined, but from the circumstance of the impracticability of even Indians travelling in certain directions, it would appear that it has several branches, one of which undoubtedly connects with the head of the N. W. branch of Indian river ; another continues parallel to the coast, and is the same which has been found only three miles back from Indian river at the parallel of cape Canaveral : a third prong joins the marshes from whence the Ocklawaha river takes its rise, while the main branch loses itself in the deep cypress swamps and lagoons that extend to the Ever-Glade morass, one arm leading most undoubtedly to the source of the Haffia or Manatee river, which originates also in a similar marsh, and flows into Spirito Santo bay.

The lands immediately on the borders of Dunn's lake are not of the first quality, but Haw creek and its numerous ramifications which are the chief supply of the lake, come through extensive savannas, which promise to be future sugar fields, and appear capable of being brought into cultivation when properly drained.

The number of settlements that once adorned the banks of St. John's river have disappeared, in consequence of the Indian wars and other causes before alluded to ; and in sailing up that majestic stream an air of stillness impresses the beholder with the idea that he is navigating the waters of an uninhabited and new country.

The future prospects we may consider as more flattering ; *for in estimating the value of our new territory, we have accounted upon what it will be when fully settled, rather than what it now is.*

Above lake George the lands though in general low, may be considered as capable of producing various lucrative articles, for the rise of the river is not of that sudden or great nature as to inundate and destroy ; and it may by trifling embankments be easily altogether prevented from flowing on the soil.

The lands on the margin of St. John's river below lake George, are hammock and swamp of all qualities, seldom more than half a mile wide ; behind this all are pine lands, both between the river and the hammocks and swamps, that run parallel to and at a small distance from the Atlantic ocean. The Twelve-mile swamp, and a few veins of good land on the large tributary creeks on each side of the river are exceptions.

The Diego plains, the hammocks and swamps of Pablo creek, North river and Guana creek, are very good lands and convenient to market. To the southward of St. Augustine, rich fertile hammocks and swamps are found on the margin of Matanzas, Halifax, Mosquito, and Indian rivers or lagoons, and upon the creeks that empty into them.

Great quantities of live oak of the largest size were once to be found, but the timber fit for the first rate vessels of war is already scarce, and so far back from navigable waters as to render its transportation nearly impracticable. It is no longer to be found to any considerable extent on the St. John's river or its tributary creeks. Some small portions yet remain on the banks of the North river, and on Diego plains, but it is feared that until a canal is made that the wood is scarcely accessible at the latter place. On Dunn's lake there is but very little ; the *present supply* is obtained only from the hammocks on Pablo creek and Halifax river. At the head of Indian. river and its branches, there is some live oak timber, but it is too remote. Cedar is very scarce and but little to be found, except upon one or two creeks on the west side of St. John's river.

Much false expectation has been raised respecting the quantity of live oak and cedar in Florida, and these observations are thrown out, more with a view of guarding the unexperienced from indulging in this supposition, than pretending to state with precision the real extent of resources in this respect.

There are many roads or paths through this eastern subdivision of St. John's county, but only two or three practicable for wheel carriages. The King's road from the Cowford to St. Augustine, and thence southwardly to the Tomoca settlements at the head of Halifax river, is now reopened by the exertions of the inhabitants residing in the neighbourhood ; and the road to the mouth of Pablo creek is at present the mail route, and generally used by visitors to St. Augustine. A carriage road also leads from the town to a landing upon the Six-mile creek, whose mouth is at Picolati, and from which landing a short canal might be made to the head of navigation on St. Sebastian's river, which flows into the harbour of St. Augustine. Were this done, which is perfectly practicable, the waters of the St. John's being thus connected with an established port, much produce would be transported to St. Augustine, whose bar at least equals that of St. John's, and a dangerous boat navigation through lake Valdez and the bay of Black creek, as well as the other wide parts of the river, would be avoided.

Roads diverge from St. Augustine to various points of the St. John's, particularly Kingsley's bluff, Julington creek, Picolati, Buena Vista old and new, Rollestown, Dunn's lake, Buffalo bluff, Volusia, Spring Garden and Beresford's ; and to the settlements at Matanzas, and on the creeks discharging there : these however at present are only bridle paths ; obscure trails lead from the Tomoca and

Volusia settlements over the head of the N. W. branch of Indian river, and thence in a southwardly course parallel to that stream. A road also goes along the sea beach from opposite to St. Augustine to the mouth of St. John's.

The Twelve-mile swamp near St. Augustine is equal to any body of land in the southern states for fertility : it appears to have been first cultivated in 1770, but since the occupancy of Florida by the Spaniards scarcely any agricultural operation there was attended to. Graham's swamp, between Matanzas inlet and Tomoca, is also a rich soil, and the fresh marshes adjacent thereto are very eligible for sugar, &c. Colonel Bulow of South Carolina and some other enterprising planters are forming settlements in and near this place, which will doubtless give a tone to the undertakings in the country.

The chain of good lands extends parallel to Halifax river and Mosquito south lagoon down to the head of Indian river. At Ross' old settlement on Mosquito lagoon sugar was formerly raised in large quantities : as also at the town of New-Smyrna ; to which a body of redemptioners from the islands of the Mediterranean were almost kidnapped ; and forced to labour until the impositions exercised upon them, compelled the unhappy bondsmen to rise on their oppressors, and they settled in St. Augustine ; where their descendants form a numerous, industrious and virtuous body of people, distinct alike from the indolent character of the Spaniard and the rapacious habits of some of the strangers who have visited that city since the exchange of flags. In their duties as small farmers, hunters, fishermen, and other laborious but useful occupations, they contribute more to the real stability of society than any other class of people : generally temperate in their mode of life, and strict in their moral integrity, they do not yield the palm to the denizens of the land of steady habits : crime is almost unknown among them ; speaking their native tongue, they move about distinguished by a primitive simplicity and honesty, as remarkable as their speech.

Of Rollestown, once an equally important settlement, not a vestige is left except a few pits which once were the foundations of large buildings, and a long avenue yet distinctly to be traced through the forests, the commencement of a grand highway to St. Augustine : the object of the founder was singular, in one respect, which contemplated the practicability of reforming the morals of a certain class of unhappy females, by transplanting them from the purlieus of Drury-lane to the solitudes of Florida.

The planters upon Tomoca river and its vicinity are almost wholly English settlers from the Bahamas, who quitting those sterile rocks, came hither to avail themselves of a better soil : all of them have prospered, and several have become very rich by raising sea-island cotton, which for some years previous to this period well repaid their labours.

As the river St. John inclines considerably to the Atlantic shore, the country to the westward of it is much wider than the eastern subdivision which has been treated of, and is perhaps under all circumstances the most interesting part of Florida. The Ocklawaha river, which is the principal branch of the St. John's, the Amasura discharging into the Gulf of Mexico, most of the streams that empty into Spirito Santo bay, Black creek a large tributary of St. John's river, all water this district, as also the eastern branches of the Santaffy.

The dividing ridge of the waters of the Atlantic ocean and the gulf of Mexico, is very irregular in its elevation ; at some places it scarcely rises into small undulations, in others it swells to considerable hills : it may perhaps more correctly be designated as a *plateau* of land ; one spur leading from the old Suwanee town, on the river of that name, runs parallel to the coast close on the west of the great Alachua savanna, where it meets another arm coming from the north-east, running between the sources of Sanfilasky and Tslachlio-saw creeks, and stretching towards the St. John's ; these united

10

proceed in a south-east course, and divide the Ocklawaha and Ami-sura rivers, and expanding very considerably have a series of Indian villages planted on them, until as they approach the vast sa⁻vannas in the south they gradually sink down to their level : branches of this ridge lie on both sides of the Amisura river, and on the north west of Spirito Santo bay. A very hilly region is also found on the neck which separates the St. John's from the Ocklawaha, and bordering close on the latter river. *Santa Fe*

The extent, from the waters of the ~~Santaffy~~ in the direction of the ridge, and extending on each side including the Alachua territory, down to the head of Spirito Santo bay ; and on the forks of the Ami-sura, and other rivers, is a beautiful undulating fertile country, containing large bodies of hammock and oak and hickory land, with pine lands of a rich soil based on limestone : over this portion of the country as in many parts of West Florida nature has scattered a number of wells, holes and ponds of all sizes and various depths, many of them sufficient with the protecting shade of the surrounding trees or bushes, to resist the exhausting evaporations produced by the fervid glow of the summer sun ; becoming reservoirs of water, cool in the warmest day. Some of these have their banks of such a slope as to allow cattle to descend to the water : others are of so perpendicular a descent as to require the use of a rope and bucket, and all are distinguished by a tuft of hammock trees growing around even the smallest, giving a pleasing variety to the monotony of the pine woods.

Handsome streams of water are found in almost all the hammocks, which on the *plateau* generally discharge into some pond or lake : many of these rivulets afford for two thirds of the year sufficient water to drive mills.

Besides the smaller ponds, a larger kind are often met with, some of which are even romantic in their appearance, particularly lake Ware, a beautiful sheet of water three miles wide and about five in length. In this lake is a beautiful island abounding with groves of the bitter-sweet or Seville orange : this was the favourite retreat of one of the antient chiefs of the aboriginal inhabitants. Lake Pithlachucco and Orange lake are in many parts deep; most of these large waters are in tempestuous weather agitated like a sea.

The great savannas are also remarkable : after periods of heavy falls of rain, they are inundated to the depth of several feet ; but when the warm seasons have evaporated this deluge, they often become so entirely dry that the fire runs over them, and sweeps down the tall grass which has sprung up over them to a great height.

The great Alachua savanna is the most considerable, being but seldom entirely free from water. Many curious stories are circulated among the Indians respecting a whirlpool, where a subterraneous discharge of water is said to take place ; but the author has not been able to ascertain the fact. A communication exists by a narrow cypress swamp, from the Alachua savanna to the head of Orange lake : this latter terminates at its eastern extremity in a thick swamp, through which its waters gradually oozing, form at length a creek, rapid and deep, but narrow and very crooked, and abounding with logs and sand bars : this water course proceeding in a north-east direction, joins the Ocklawaha river. Ockawilla and Chicuchaty savannas are very considerable, particularly the latter.

In speaking of the hammocks it should be observed, that they in general surround the large lakes and savannas, though also found scattered over the whole face of the country like islets : within them however a pond or lake is generally found, and often their size is regulated by the extent of this watery nucleus. On the exterior of the hammocks the black oak and hickory land is disposed and gradually spreads to the pine ridges, on which the hickory is often found. The pine lands however are not all of the same elevated character : many of them being flat and covered with gall berry and huckle berry bushes : and sometimes interspersed with cypress ponds and bay galls : these however are always in the vicinity of the sources of the streams, and are but rarely found on the *plateau;* but nevertheless like all the pine ranges, they afford excellent pasturage for cattle, and if sown with the artificial grasses would procure abundant crops.

It may be here remarked of the pine lands in general of Florida, that they are fertile ; a character strictly applicable, although they seem to the superficial view unfit for agriculture, particularly to the eye of a northern farmer who from early association of ideas, considers pine lands and barrenness as terms synonymous. Luxuriant pasture ranges are found every where, and millions of horned cattle may be raised with no other trouble than herding and periodically burning the grass, which quickly grows again, the tender shoots imparting by their succulency and fragrance, a flavour to the flesh not always found in the stall-fed beeves of a city. The chief support of the antient Indian population was derived from their countless herds of cattle, which a succession of invasions from hostile tribes and lawless borderers have now almost wholly exterminated.

The Amanina river is a beautiful stream, and flows through a tract equal to any in these parts; and but for the impediment of the shallows at its mouth, would afford a great outlet for produce ; as it is, small craft will convey the exports to the great emporium of Spirito Santo bay.

The Ocklawaha river takes its rise in lake Eustis, which like the head lagoon of St. John's river, is formed by the accumulation of waters from the great southern marshes. Its course is parallel to the St. John's, and it occasionally expands into lakes as flowing through the alluvial soil on its banks. As its course diverges to the east to fall into the St. Johns, the vast volumes of water brought with rapidity down its narrow channel overflow the low lands, and a labyrinth of islands intervene, from where the Orange lake creek joins it, to its junction with the principal stream some miles below

lake George. These islands are covered with a luxuriant growth
of tall swamp trees, but so entirely inundated as to make their redemption for cultivation a Herculean task : but which once ef-
fectually accomplished, would make them mines of wealth, unequalled perhaps by the best Missisippi sugar fields.

The high lands between the St. John's and Ocklawaha rivers, south
of the path from the Volunia to the Indian crossing places, are of the
same character with those of the *plateau* on the western side of the latter stream. North of the above path, large veins of scrubs extend to
lake George and chiefly fill up the neck. These scrubs and undulating grounds, consist of a sand of a very small and ferruginous
grain, producing an infinite variety of dwarf oaks and a number of
parasitical plants ; where the land swells to a considerable elevation,
there is generally to be seen a growth of small spruce pines, most of
which however seem to die, after springing up to the height of
twenty or thirty feet. The wythes and other creeping shrubs which
interweave with the humble species of oaks, render a passage very
difficult, and the paths which are so directed as to cross the scrubs in
the narrowest part, wind so to take advantage of the intervals between the patches of bushes. Water is very scarce here, and only
found in a few sinks or ponds similar to those in the pine lands, but
without trees around them. Another kind of land, are the ridges of
white sand covered with the small black or post oak, commonly called black jacks. These are sometimes so thick as to exclude the
pines, and when this is the case there is scarcely any grass found on
the sand hills.

On the southwestern part of the Alachua territory, and extending between the Amasura river and the Mexican gulf is a remarkable tract of country, which presents a curious appearance : the
whole of the pine lands, which are remarkably handsome from
their undulating surfaces, were burnt some thirty years since ;
instead of the clear open woods generally seen, masses of young

pine saplings are thickly spread over the rocky ground, which is strewn with half burnt light wood logs, that have not been destroyed by the action of the air for so many years, while numerous still more hardy pieces of timber remain erect though dead, firm as adamant pillars. Here and there a solitary green pine remains that escaped the ravages of the original fire, which succeeded by almost annual ones, have kept the woods in a state of continual undergrowth. It is supposed that a space of nearly three hundred square miles have been thus devastated, and nothing can be more desolate than the situation of a traveller who bewildered in this labyrinth, roams without end over mossy rocks and shaking morasses, impeded at every step by the black shapeless logs ; at every eminence he sees the same scene repeated, and no end appears to this very remarkable desert.

Here and in many other neighboring parts of the extensive *plateau*, rocks are found upon the surface, of every size ; sometimes loose, or disposed in curious ridges that to a fanciful imagination, give the idea of the irregular rootings of mammoth swine : these rocks and stones consist of a sileceous nucleus, enveloped in successive laminæ of different formations of lime-stone : there are even occasionally met with something resembling mill or burr-stones, well adapted for sharpening tools and grinding corn. Clay too is found here and in many other parts of these western pine lands. The general soil may be described as consisisting of a light but rich loamy sand.

It may be mentioned here, being omitted inadvertently in its proper place, that a similar scene of devastation exists on the main path from the old Suwanee to the Mikasukie towns, though produced by a different cause. Many years since, a tornado passed over the lands there and prostrated for leagues every tree : so sudden and so universal was the effect of the ruin, that immense numbers of the deer and other wild animals were crushed to death, besides herds of cattle : the Indians and Indian negroes state that the bones of the beasts thus suddenly destroyed are to be seen scattered in every direction, and it has been asserted, that it is only within latter years that the trees have rotted away sufficiently, to allow horses to travel along the paths which are thus incumbered.

It is within the subdivision of St. John's county now under description, that a large number of the grants and patents issued since 1812 are ordered to be located : the great Alachua grant to Arredondo and Sons of the Havana, and several other extensive patents are here : and a part of the purchase of Hackley under the Duke of Alagon is included in this ; more particular notice of which and the other, will be taken in another part of the work.

The paths through this portion of Florida are numerous : the main routes from the Suwanee meet in the centre of the Alachua at the town of Micanopy, on the northern bank of Taskawilla lake ; from hence which was the antient capital of the Indian nation, the tracts diverge in all directions to Black creek, Picolati, Vibrilia and Buffalo bluff on the central parts of St. John's river : routes also go down to Tampa bay through the chain of Indian villages and settlements, and to the lower crossing places over the Ocklawaha by way of lake Ware, and hence a path leads to Volusia on the St. John's above lake George. It is by this latter course that the mail is said to have been ordered to travel from Pensacola ; but why it should be sent nearly one hundred miles from the straight direction it is difficult to determine : after crossing the Suwanee river it ought to pass through Micanopy, and thence either to Vibrilia and new Buena Vista on the St. John's, where there is a good ferry established, and on to St. Augestine : or from Micanopy to Picolati lower down the river. The former route would at present be better, as the stages would be more regularly divided ; though in either case, three days easy journey, without travelling by night, would bring the mail from the Suwanee to St. Augustine.

Several roads from the eastward and northward meet at Chicucha-ty, and thence go down to the falls on the Haffia. In the northern part, paths proceed from Black creek, Picolati, and the Cowford, di-rect to the upper part of the Suwanee.

It is across this part of Florida that at some no distant time a com-munication will be established for travellers to New-Orleans. Steam boats coming direct from the large northern cities, will enter the St. John's and proceed up to some eligible landing, and the passen-gers taking stages to the banks of the Suwanee near its mouth, will again embark in these ambulating hotels, and proceed along the shores of the Gulf of Mexico to New-Orleans : by this route a voyage from New-York to the former city may be easily completed in ten days.

Connecting the waters of Black creek and Santaffy rivers by a navagable canal of thirty or forty miles a route may be opened, that will afford many facilities for bringing the produce that comes down to Appalachie bay, to the Atlantic markets, and of conveying the re-turns : independent of the fruits of the plantations for many miles around the canal.

The junction of the Ocklawaha and Amisura rivers would require a shorter cut, but from the high lands is impracticable in such a country : the former river however is navigable almost to its very source, and will serve as a channel of exportation of all the agricul-tural productions that do not find their outlet by Spirito Santo bay, through the St. John's.

This portion of Florida which the author has endeavoured to de-lineate, contains nearly all the most valuable lands in the territory, and may be accounted healthy in almost every spot : the general elevation of the land and the openness of the woods, allows a free circulation of the air, set in motion by the winds from either side of the peninsula, and uncontaminated by the exhalations from intermin-able swamps, and endless bodies of low land.

We now proceed to examine the remaining two subdivisions, into which the county of St. John has been distributed in relation to our subject, being all the lands lying below the parallel of the twenty-eighth degree of latitude, considering as before mentioned, the chain of low lands as a division between the Atlantic and Mexican districts, commencing near the head of St. John's river and terminating at the mouth of Shark river or cape Sable creek.

The western part of this descriptive subdivision is exclusively occupied by the remainder of the purchase of Hackley from the Duke of Alagon alluded to a few pages back : included within these limits are the three spacious and celebrated harbors of Tampa, Charlotte and Chatham bays, besides a variety of rivers the mouths of which afford inlets for small coasting vessels. Tampa or more properly Spirito Santo bay has been described in a former part of these topographical observations : it may be remarked in addition here that there are two other inlets besides the principal one, each affording from twelve to eighteen feet at low water. The coast generally between Spirito Santo bay and Charlotte harbor is composed of flat islands in front of high forests of pine, behind which there is reason to believe the country is chequered with similar masses of hammock disposed over an undulating region of fertile pine lands as are found upon the plateau in the north and western parts of this country : the auther however has not been able with all diligent research to find any existing record of a description of this tract : and consequently no detail is laid down of it, and but few water courses appear on the map, but when minute information can be procured, it will undoubtedly be found well supplied in that respect. The banks of Asternal and Charlotte rivers as well as those of the Coolasahatchie and Delaware are well wooded with excellent timber.

All along this coast down to cape Romano or Punta Larga, the tide ebbs and flows only once in twenty four hours with a rise of but three feet : this is increased or diminished according to the preva-

11

lence of the winds in the gulf of Mexico : in dry seasons the tide rises high in the fresh water rivers being perceptible at some distance from the sea. In Chatham bay the tide ebbs and flows what is called tide and half tide : that is three hours flood and three hours ebb : then nine hours flood and nine hours ebb : the current of the tide is very rapid, and the rise is seven feet as far as the point of cape Romano, beyond which its influence is not felt.

From the head of Chatham bay to cape Sable creek, numbers of small islands and keys line the coast and several small streams empty. Pavilion keys and Lostman's keys are the principal, and like the rest as well as the generality of the land on the main, consist of drowned mangrove swamps.

On the margin of some of the small waters, are hills of a rich soil which rise among these dreary mangroves, and from the traces of antient cultivation yet visible on many of them, were probably the last retreats of the Coloosa nation of Indians which has long been extinct, having been gradually driven from the country by other tribes. The pine lands behind these swamps are computed to be at a distance of ten miles from the coast across the mangroves, and beyond the narrow ridge they occupy, comes the great Ever-glade morass.

Scarcely any paths through this subdivision are known except the one leading from the falls of the Haffia or Manatee : these falls are merely rapids over a bed of secondary limestone rocks, determining the head of navigation of that river. This path inclines in a south east direction, and traverses the great chain of low lands and the prongs of the glades at the narrow parts, known only to a few of the most wandering of the Indians ; after many days travelling in water, during which they carry with them prepared provisions and stakes to raise them above the level of the inundation while resting, they find their way to the Atlantic coast somewhere about Jupiter inlet.

The vast bodies of low lands that lie south of this trail and fill up

the interior of the southern extremity of the Florida peninsula, appears
to have scattered over it many tracts of firm land in the form of
islands and promontories, and though at present a communication
across appears impracticable, and the accounts from Indians, negroes
and refugee whites, place it in the worst possible point of view, yet it
is by no means improbable there is a passage from island to island, over
the several branches of the morass which are not always of a breadth
to deter the attempt : nay the author is more inclined to believe, that
from the general exaggeration human nature is prone to, it may be better than supposed, and that if the discouraging accounts do not deter
a sectional survey, it is by no means problematical but the expense
would be amply repaid by the discovery of many rich pieces of land
in detached spots : how far admitting them to be found, settlers would
be induced to purchase on supposed unhealthy situations need scarcely be discussed : where the profits are proportionate every risk has
been and will continue to be hazarded, by the spirit of enterprise
which in this country is so predominant ; which leads the hunter to
seek his valuable skins in the frozen mountain of the north west, and
sends the agriculturist and merchant to the remotest and most unhealthy places.

The Atlantic subdivision of the southern part of St. John's county has almost wholly been described while treating on the general
outline of the Florida coast, for nothing is known of the interior except what has been stated in that place ; the rivers along the whole
length from north to south, appearing to head in the Ever-glade morass or branches connected with it. Some difference exists between
St. Lucie as it was found by the author, and the description given by
Romans, who states that he went up the N. W. branch that appearing
the principal, for twenty-four miles reckoning direct distance ; that
there the river became narrow and partly on account of the obstruc-
tion of the logs, partly on account of the rapidity of the stream, he
left the vessel and going up by land found the river at last to run

through a vast plain, the bank of the stream being fringed with a few trees. When this account is compared with what was observed by the writer and stated in a former part of this work, he is tempted to consider with Sir Walter Raleigh, that if the same place and circumstances is viewed by different persons under such contrary aspects, that he had better burn his book and avoid the risk of being considered the narrator of untruths. That however there is some great reservoir of water is certain, from the profusion of fresh water which the river St. Lucie pours down : such is the immense quantity that the whole sound is often made fresh through its vast extent and deep indentations.

The rapid current of the gulf stream sweeping close along this part of the Florida coast has the effect of closing the bars of the inlets, particularly Jupiter, through which so immense a volume of water seeks to discharge itself, that nothing but the continued throwing up of the loose sea shells prevents the streams from forcing it open : they even sometimes prevail : Jupiter inlet after a heavy freshet in the spring of 1769 was opened and so remained for three or four years. On Indian river inlet the freshets sometimes make ten feet water and at other periods there are not three : the general quantity found is five feet. The bar of Rio Seco is similarly closed to Jupiter, and also a small inlet called Indian creek near cape Florida.

Cayo Largo though ranked among the Florida keys is no more than a promontory from the main land about half distance between capes Florida and Sable, and connected by a very narrow isthmus : the whole however is rather a cluster of mangroves than solid land, except where the gulf washes up a sandy beach on the exterior. Sound point or Cayo Largo was formerly called cape Florida, but that name is now applied to the eastern part of key Biscayne.

The topographical observations on the continental part of Florida, as far as correct information has been procured, being thus concluded we should proceed to the subject of the keys and banks, known under the designation of the general Florida reef, but as their capabilities are confined to maritime concerns, and an interesting account of the wrecking system and other similar points are closely interwoven with them, we shall defer entering on this branch of our subject for the present.

OBSERVATIONS ON THE SOIL AND ITS NATURAL GROWTH.

The general character of the Florida lands is light : sands of different granulations, and sandy loams based upon limestone or clay at a variety of depth, are what chiefly are found ; and from this lightness they are perhaps not capable of bearing a succession of exhausting crops ; but nevertheless the land when thrown into *old fields* soon renovates itself, from a fertilizing principle which pervades the air, and subsides to the earth : this principle is undoubtedly generated by the saline particles, which are carried from each sea on to the lands.

The different qualities of land in the Floridas, may be divided decidedly into, and known under the following names :

Flat pine lands	Pine land savannas
Undulating pine lands	Hammock savannas
Low hammock	River swamps
High hammock	Cypress swamps
Oak and hickory lands	Fresh marshes
Scrub lands	Salt marshes

The *flat pine lands* are of themselves of two kinds : the one sort covered with a thick and luxuriant growth of berry bushes, dwarf bays and laurels, with grass only in patches, and the pine trees sparsely scattered over the ground : the other kind has little or no undergrowth: being thickly covered with savannas and cypress ponds and galls, it is often overflown from them and on the least fall of rain becomes drowned ; the herbage however is generally plentiful. It is with these two sorts of low piny land, that a great portion of this space between the sea and St. John's river is covered, mixed in however often with the other descriptions of soil, but giving on the first view an unfavorable idea to the new comer; a great number of branches and runs of water take their rise among these low grounds ; and wherever these low pine lands are found they may be considered as the head of some river or creek.

The *elevated and undulating pine lands* are healthy and beautiful ; the timber is taller, straighter and of a better quality than on the low grounds : their appearance in the western part of the country has been already described, and wherever they are met with partake more or less of that nature : they abound with succulent herbage : the *Saw palmetto* bushes are very rarely found in these high pine lands, they being confined to a middling description of ground not so low as to be liable to frequent inundations, nor high enough to foster a different species of undergrowth.

The *low hammocks* are the richest kind of lands in Florida, and capable of producing for many successive years rich crops of sugar, corn, hemp, or other equally exhausting productions : they are however clothed with so heavy a growth of timber and underwood, that the task of clearing them is appalling, and they require ditching and banking to guard them from extraordinary floods and rains.

Graham's swamp, between Matanzas and Tomoco, is chiefly low hammock. The upper parts of both sides of Indian river and its north-west branch are of this quality of soil, as also the margins of the river St. John from Volusia to Beresford's old cowpen, though narrow and perhaps somewhat too low. Many fine tracts of low hammock are scattered over the western parts of the peninsula, about the heads of the Santaffy and other rivers, and on the banks of Alligator creek and many of the smaller tributary streams ; also in the upper part of the region between the Suwanee and Appalachicola rivers.

Here and elsewhere, West Florida *proper* is scarcely mentioned ; for confined between the Perdido and the Appalachicola rivers, it is so comparatively small and but little known, that it has not been taken into consideration. It is true that to magnify its importance, a " *monstrous cantle*" has been carved out of East Florida ; but in the subsequent pages of this book, it should be understood that East Florida comprehends all to the *East* of the Appalachicola river, including in fact seven eighths of the whole territory.

The growth of timber usual on these low hammocks is principally the cabbage tree, (of which it may be observed in passing, that none are found west of the Ocklockonne river) ash, mulberry, dogwood, Spanish oak, live oak, white oak, swamp hickory, sweet bay, sassafras, cedar, magnolia, wild fig, wild orange, zantoxyhim or prickley ash, and a vast number of other kinds, with varieties of all : in the more southern latitudes the torch tree is found, also the gum guiacum, mastic, wild tamarind, red stopper, pigeon plum, cocoa plum, sea grape, tiswood, &c. &c. A thick vegetable mould of from one to two feet in depth, covers the surface of the ground in these low hammocks, below which black coarse sand is found, gradually becoming paler as the depth increases, until the clay or limestone is struck.

The *high hammocks* are if possible more dense in their growth than the others, but the coat of vegetable matter is thin, and the white sand lies within a foot or eighteen inches of the surface :

they are said to be notwithstanding very productive for years, without any manure, which indeed is never thought of being applied.

In addition to most of the trees found in the low hammocks, we meet laurel, red oak, chestnut oak, chinquopine, beech, persimmon, cinnamon-laurel, bastard-ash, myrtle, locust, and a numerous list of other trees : great varieties of the cane and reed are in both descriptions of hammocks : countless parasitical plants interweave and fold round the trees ; the wild vine shoots up to a most surprising height, and the stalk is commonly found seven and eight inches in diameter.

The *oak and hickory lands* produce almost exclusively those two kinds of forest trees, with occasionally gigantic pines : the underbrush is generally composed of sucker saplings of the oak and hickory ; this description of land is generally disposed on the exterior edges of the high hammocks, and separate them from the pine lands. The black oak is the species most general here ; the soil a rich deep yellow sandy loam.

The *scrub lands* have been particularly described before in page 77 <del>88</del> they vary but very little in their general appearance wherever found, and are of too forbidding an aspect to lead the farmer to expect from them any advantage, except perhaps that of raising hogs, for which they are peculiarly well adapted, from the abundance of acorns on the dwarf oaks, and a number of curious roots to the sandy plants.

The *pine land savannas* have a very black and rich appearance, but notwithstanding they contain only white sands, though the clay beneath is perhaps nearer the surface ; they are merely sinks or drains to the higher grounds, their low situation preventing the growth of pines. Most of the roads in the vicinity of St. Augustine are unfortunately obliged to traverse very extensive regions of this sort, and consequently in wet seasons they are scarcely passable, and greatly disgust the transient visitor.

12

The *hammock savannas* have a more fertile soil; fossil broken shells, are embedded in the mould which is rich and black, and of some depth : the clay is often within a foot of the surface of the earth. The great Alachua savanna, the savannas on the borders of Haw creek and its prongs, and the large savannas west of and parallel to Indian river, are of this description : deep ditching and high banking will be however requisite, to guard them from the inundations their low position naturally exposes them to. Pasturage of the most luxuriant kind is afforded by these savannas, which are valuable features in the territory.

The word *swamp* is, in the signification now adopted, peculiar to America ; by it is understood a tract of land lying low, but with a sound bottom, covered in rainy seasons and high waters with that element. Almost all forest trees, pines excepted, thrive best in the swamps, where the soil is rich, and when capable of being cleared and drained they are proper for the growth of rice, sugar, corn, hemp, indigo, &c. &c.

The *river swamps* are annually overflown, and require judicious and indefatigable attention to their embankments when in a state of cultivation. The growth common in these swamps are the swamp oak, willow oak, swamp maple, tupelo, elder, willow, swamp magnolia, black birch, sumac, cypress, black and white poplar, Florida holly; sycamore, hawthorn, &c. &c. Sometimes the land immediately on the river banks is rather higher than the grounds a little behind, which are then called back swamps ; these are nearly constantly full of water, and have chiefly tupelo growth, and no underwood.

Cypress swamps are mostly near the heads of rivers, and in a continued state of inundation ; little or no underbrush, but only crowds of the cypress shoots or *knees*, which point up like small pyramids. In the river St. John many of the swamps and islands are of this kind, as also in the lower parts of the Ocklawaha ; they are likewise bordering on the great southern morasses in every direction.

While we are on the subject of wooded low lands it may be observed, that in the pine lands, the early courses of the creeks and streams are through two sorts of channels, *bay galls* and *cypress galls.* The *bay galls* are spongy, boggy, and treacherous to the foot, with a coat of matted vegetable fibres : the loblolly bays spread their roots, and the saw palmetto crawls on the ground, making them altogether unpleasant and even dangerous to cross : the water in these bay galls is strongly impregnated with pyroligneous acid. The *cypress galls* have firm sandy bottoms, and are only troublesome from the multitude of the sprouting knees. Clay is often found in both these kinds of galls, which are sometimes very narrow and sometimes dilate into large morasses.

The *fresh water marshes* are of two kinds, *hard* and *soft* ; the *hard marsh* is made up of a kind of marly clay whose soil has too much solidity for the water to disunite its particles : and therefore, being also generally higher above the water, may be with little trouble adapted to proper cultivation : the *soft marshes* lie lower and are more subject to overflow and require in the embankments, earth from the high land to make them substantial, and consequently are more expensive in their redemption ; but this once accomplished they are undoubtedly the most fruitful ; affording in the dry culture means of raising sugar, hemp, corn, cotton and indigo.

The *salt marshes* are likewise of two kinds, *hard* and *soft*, from the same causes that effect the fresh marsh : the *hard salt marshes* however are often altogether clay, and like those in Indian river are covered with purslain : these when fully embanked and redeemed, and freshened by the cultivation of cotton or hemp for a year or two, would undoubtedly become the finest sugar fields : that hard kind of salt marsh upon which fresh water occasionally flows and known commonly as *rush land*, is extremely eligible when properly prepared for agricultural purposes.

The *soft salt marshes* are totally useless except as manure : in the part of the peninsula south of Musquito, the mangrove takes the place of the marsh grass and reeds, and by its interlacing roots give^s a greater consistence to the soil : when the main stem of a mangrove bush or tree gains a little height it sends down to the water a new shoot or root, and each horizontal branch as it puts forth, does the same, by which the parent trunk is surrounded, like the East Indian Banyan tree : these downward shoots as they approach the water branch into several points, which again subdivide almost *ad infinitum*, until the family of roots are twice as numerous as the upper branches, thickly set together, extending in all directions, and closely interwoven with the similar ramifications from the surrounding trees or bushes, often causing the *growing up* of the channel of a narrow creek, whose waters in times of freshets and floods ooze through their roots as through a thousand miniature arches.

It may be observed generally of the soil of Florida, that there are four strata : the upper coat of vegetable mould or earth : below sand ; beyond that marl or clay; and lowest of all indurations of shell and limestone rocks. This arrangement is however by no means constant; there are frequent bluffs on the St. John's, particularly at Volusia, which are high and covered deep with a rich loamy black sand thickly overspread and mingled with broken fossil, and periwinkle shells in every state of perfection, and below this is only sand : other varieties from the general rule are continually found. However this may partially be, it seems certain, that the two harder substrata retain the moisture from oozing through the sands, and thus become another cause of fertility.

It has been a matter of some question whether the orange is an indigene of Florida, but after a due consideration of the question it would appear it is not ; for although now found in almost every swamp and hammock, yet it is only where the wandering Indians may have scattered the seeds : in those places where they have not been at all seasons of the year, though far south, the orange is seldom if ever found ; where man has not penetrated with the fruit in his hand it is unknown. The kind of orange most common in the Florida woods is the sour and bitter-sweet : of these latter some are almost as free from acid as a China orange, and retain only enough of the aromatic bitter, to make them in the taste of many superior to the sweet orange itself. A most delicious wine is made in England of the Seville orange, which appears to be the same that is called the bitter-sweet : the numerous groves of this fruit in Florida will one day when the sugar is plentiful, induce the farmer to adopt orange wine as a pleasant, healthful and economical domestic beverage.

The wild grapes of Florida when duly trained and cultivated, will afford another simple fermented drink : let us hope that the dreadful practice of drinking ardent spirits may be checked in our new territory, and that the more sober juice of the grape and orange may supersede the use of those intoxicating draughts, which in many parts of our union threaten almost to brutalize the human being and degrade him beyond redemption.

The myrtle wax shrub is found in every part of the Floridas ; the berries are gathered in a vessel and bruised and then boiled : the wax is skimmed off and when cold is of a dull green : from this candles are made : it may however be bleached by various simple chemical processes ; in many parts of Carolina and Georgia the planters use lights of this wax altogether.

The gall nuts which in our druggist shops bear a high price, are commonly found on the dwarf oaks among the scrub lands in every part of the country.

Hops are said by Romans to be indigenous in Florida, but the author did not meet with any. In Sweden formerly a strong cloth was made from the stalks of hops, which required however a much longer time to be steeped in water than flax.

The starry aniseed or somo, or skimmi of Japan and China has been found indigenous in Florida : and many other plants of that country are also natives here: whence we may infer that others, productive in commerce, may be profitably introduced.

Almost all the natural vegetable productions of Florida may be advantageously turned to account by the industrious, and time will develope the mode in which it is to be done : at present we can only point out those more immediately prominent, and proceed to another division of our subject, having in this one merely aimed at giving a stranger a more distinct idea of the soil and growth of our territory and enabling him to judge for himself. Again however it is deemed incumbent to warn those who are unacquainted with the subject, from condemning the vast tracts of pine lands in Florida to neglect, for in the end they will be found to yield perhaps the most satisfactory returns : it may be said " do not visit Florida with high raised expectations of fertility or you will be disappointed" : but it must be added. " and on the contrary, do not suppose every pine tract a barren, or that sterility is a consequent attendant on our light soils and sandy regions."

OBSERVATIONS UPON THE SEVERAL APPRO-PRIATE ARTICLES OF CULTURE.

The great expectations which have been raised respecting Flori-da, have included within their range a hope of introducing many if not all of the richest of the West India productions, particularly coffee, and it even led to the projected formation of a company in Philadelphia for that purpose, who fitted out an expedition in July 1821 to explore the country and select eligible spots for the future cultivation of the coffee plant : the results of this expedition have never been published, but reports of a nature most favorable to the scheme were afloat twelve months since : they have however gradu-ally died away, and if the project has not been abandoned, it waits at least a more auspicious moment for completion, congress having refused to grant a peremptive right of purchase to a company, of lands stated to be eligible for the purposes intended.

From the preceding pages the reader has not perhaps been im-pressed with such sanguine expectations respecting the coffee plant, and the author without pretending to negative the assertion of the practicability of raising this berry, does not think it can be recom-

mended as a safe speculation, for reasons stated in other places.
Sea Island cotton, Cuba tobacco, sugar and a numerous list of fruits,
marketable both in a green and preserved state, surely are productions in themselves sufficiently lucrative to draw the attention of the
planter, and to these will he confined what follows on the subject of
cultures appropriate to Florida.

Respecting cotton, it has been so profitable to every Florida planter who has raised and prepared it for market, as done in the southern states, that it may only be slightly mentioned. The resident
gentlemen on Amelia, Talbot and fort George islands, at Pablo, at
Matanzas and at Tomoco have cultivated it for many years, and their
brands have ever commanded the first prices in the markets of Savannah and Charleston, particularly those of our respected delegate Joseph M. Hernandez, Esq. from his plantation *Mala Compra*
at Matanzas ; of which, by the bye, it may be remarked, that the soil
(high hammock) is now as white and as sandy as the beach of the
Atlantic, and yet most luxuriant crops are annually produced. Here
and at other plantations exists a practice of cutting down the old
cotton stalks and suffering the shoots therefrom to spring up, which
yield with but little trouble a cotton no ways inferior to the first
crop : this is called *ratoon* cotton. Many of the fields at Tomoco
are equally white and equally fertile with those of *Mala Compra*,
and this singular appearance is found in very many other parts of
Florida, where the original growth has been almost exclusively
live oak.

Respecting sugar, the recent successful trials that have been made
upon it, have determined the curious fact that it will grow in almost
any of the soils of Florida, south of th mouth of St. John's river :
the great length of summer, or period of absolute elevation of the
thermometer above the freezing point, allows the cane to ripen
much higher than in Louisiana : it is perhaps the fact that the exhausting vegetation of this article may not allow a profitable planting

of it upon the same lands more than two or three years in succession, yet as it may be raised on the pine lands, a change of fields is easy, and attended with but little comparative trouble ; and by suffering the lands to lie fallow, or by a judicious succession of crops, it will not require a very extensive tract to establish a sugar plantation.

Perhaps it may be thought that Florida presents but little to tempt the large sugar planter : granted, but it is undoubted that if the culture of the cane should be adopted on a small scale, by the same proportionate number of cultivators that are in the habit of raising cotton in Carolina, Georgia and Alabama, their labour would be amply repaid, and a source of wealth be opened, particularly should some public spirited and enterprising individuals establish, on central and eligible points sugar mills to receive the small crops, precisely on the same principle that cotton gins and rice mills exist in the southern states. This would augment the population and increase the resources of the country sooner, and better perhaps, than any other mode. A race of independent respectable farmers would create society and happiness among themselves, and prove the back-bone of the new territory.

The fruit culture of every kind will in time become general, but although highly eligible and certainly lucrative, it will require the success of a few capitalists to give the tone to the general opinion on this head. The necessity of waiting four or five years before returns upon the principal can be made, will deter many from attending to this important branch.

It is upon the poorest spots of land, unfit for almost any thing else, that many of the numerous subsequent list of fruits may be brought into cultivation : this mode is one that requires little hard labour and exposure to noontide suns ; it can and will be adopted by a large number of the poorer class of persons, who now.inhabit the *middle country* in Georgia and North and South Carolina : these industrious people, who are obliged to toil incessantly to raise a

13

few stalks of cotton, the produce of which barely supplies half their winter clothing, will find in the warmer latitudes of Florida a pleasant employment, that will more than triple their returns in their present state of living.

Another concomitant advantage attendant on the raising and cultivation of fruit will be the circumstance of being able to do it *without slaves*. If this be properly fostered, we shall only find negroes wanted by the planter of sugar, cotton and tobacco, while a generation of industrious whites will grow up whose simple manners and virtuous habits will resemble the vine cutters and olive dressers of France and Spain; but free as the air, their unshackled independence will render them doubly happier than those almost still feudal peasants; and as a body they will prevent the possibility of those commotions which have lately threatened more than one slaveholding state.

It is a well known fact that in West Florida the French government ordered a suppression of the vineyards, lest their success might injure those in France; and we learn that similar restrictions as to the olive, and perhaps the grape, were imposed by the Spaniards over the Florida colonies. Although these decrees are antient, and have perhaps long become dead letters, yet they must have prevented the spirit of enterprise, that in the first instance suggested such establishments, which once quenched, was not easily revived.

The native grape of Florida is so very luxuriant, and circumstances shewing the practicability of planting vineyards with success, let us hope an effort may be made to introduce with judgment some of the most approved foreign grapes, which may be tried by graft, by sucker, or by seed.

The Corinthian grape, (*vitis apyrena*) or the grocers' currants of the stores, is an article of great consumption, and flourishing in the Levant, must infallibly succeed in Florida.

The great demand for dried raisins, both in boxes and jars, can surely be supplied from our own territory. We will not in the first instance pretend to rival the wines of the Rhine, the Rhone, the Loire or the Garonne ; to supersede the produce of Oporto, Xeres, Sicily or Madeira, but at least we can, after furnishing the deserts for the table of the opulent, provide a pleasant beverage for those who do not choose the products of such expensive vintages, and who will not be dissatisfied to exchange French brandy, New-England rum, or apple whiskey, for the less exciting but more palatable wines of their own country : North Carolina has proved that from their native grapes a delicious wine may be prepared, and can we doubt our success in a still more genial climate ?

The following list of productions capable of being raised in Florida, has been made out with some pains, and it is believed all these stated are profitable and practicable articles.

China orange	The olive
Madarin orange	The Vine in all its varieties
Maltese orange	Corinthian grape, or
St. Michael orange	Zante currants
Myrtle orange	Pine apple
Lemon	Fig
Lime	Plantain
Citron	Banana
Shaddock	Yam
Mangoe	Bread fruit
Pawpaw	Arrow root
Cocoa	Gall nuts
Date	Dolichos, or Soy bean
Sweet almond	Jalap
Bitter almond	True rhubarb
Tamarind	Ginger
Pistaccio	Gum gleni
Acagua	Gum guiacum

Aloe	Fustic
Cinnamon	Braziletto
Pimento	Sassafras
Sago palm	Balsam tree
Red pepper	Senna
Saponeka	Sarsaparilla
Jesuits bark	Hemp
Benne oil	Turkey madder
Palma christi oil	True opium poppy
Tea	Camphire tree
Sugar	Balm of Gilead tree
Cuba tobacco	Tumerick
Rice	Frankincense
Cotton	Cloves, Pepper
Silk	Nutmegs
Cork oak	Leechee plant of China
Chesnut tree	Liquid amber

These and a number of other articles particularly the gums, may be produced in most parts of the peninsula ; and upon looking over the list it cannot be denied that if but a little were introduced how much should we gain and how advantageous would be our prospects. Having spoken already of the vine and cotton, let us in turn consider each staple article of importance.

The Cuba tobacco has already been raised in the neighborhood of St. Augustine from seeds supplied from the Havana : the second year it however degenerates : this appears no obstacle since the seed can be procured with the greatest facility, it being very small and light : and in the lower latitndes the plant may be cultivated without such frequent renewal. If we can produce in Florida by these means a tobacco equal to the best from Cuba, it will be a great desideratum. To perfect the fragrance of the leaf, the *vanilla* which is found indigenous all over the country lends its ready aid, and *cigar*

should ~~sogar~~ smoking still continue in fashion, the *Florida weed* may in time be thought equally good with the best *Cabanas.*

It is to the olive that the patriot, the merchant and the agriculturist will look for permanent and substantial advantages to result to Florida ; the olive, favorite of Minerva, fertilized the plains of Attica, and saw young Freedom thrive beneath its shade : from the earliest time to the present eventful era, the olive has brought plenty to the regions where it was fostered, and when even liberty had passed away, remained to support and comfort the unhappy enslaved beings, whose ancestors had planted it in happier times.

It is not necessary here to describe the olive tree and its fruit, the process by which the pulp yields its oil, or the mode of preserving the *drupe :* the inquisitive reader is referred to Michaux's North American Sylva, where under the head Olive, he will find an elegant description from the classical pen of Augustus Hillhouse, an enlightened citizen of the United States, whose residence in the country of its cultivation and his literary researches, have enabled him to describe all its usefulness : a few slight abstracts are made from his pamphlet, published in Paris, that are considered interesting.

There are more than thirty varieties of the European olive tree, distinguished by their temperament as to soil and climate and the qualities of the fruit Some of their varieties, like those of the vine, owe their characteristic properties to the scene in which they are reared : Among the principal are,

The *weeping olive,* endurant of cold rather than of drought ; its branches are pendent like those of the weeping willow : its fruit and oil are pure and good.

The *round olive* is also hardy, requiring a moist good soil ; its oil is of a superior quality.

The *small round olive* requires dry and elevated grounds.

The *picholine olive* yields the most celebrated pickled olives : this variety is not delicate in the choice of soil and climate.

The olives should for Florida, be raised from the seed sown in the spring : in a year they will have attained to a height of two or three feet : in the third spring with proper attention they will be four or five feet in height and half an inch in diameter, with a *top* root of thirty inches : they should then be transplanted and placed three feet apart ; and at the end of five years may be permanently placed in the olive grove, at a distance of about forty feet : the young olives begin to yield fruit the tenth year and are fully productive about the twenty or twenty-fifth. The olive arrived to an advanced age may be transplanted in the same manner as the young tree.

This mode of raising the olive may be censured and rejected : the length of time which must elapse before they begin to reward the labor of the planter seem to forbid the adoption, more particularly by an American, who however he may persevere in an object once undertaken, would probably droop, did he foresee that he must not expect to reap the fruit of his own labours : an American particularly in a new country labors for himself and not for his son, whom he expects when arrived at maturity will equally labor : this principle is to be lamented, and may prevent the planting of other fruits as well as the olive ; but as respects the latter, could this objection to obtaining plants from the seed be overcome, it is doubtless the most eligible practice, as the plants thus reared begin a new life, they are more vigorous, of longer duration, and better adapted to a new climate than offsets from an old tree : they form also a perpendicular root which penetrates deeply and secures them from the danger of suffering by drought.

With the nicest economy in the process the weight of the expressed oil is equal to about one third of the ripe fruit : the mean produce of a tree in Florida may be assumed at thirty pounds weight of oil : though in fruitful years in Italy three hundred weight have been known to be obtained from a single tree.

The constant breezes which traverse the Florida peninsula would refresh the languid olive tree through the sultry summer, while in these southern latitudes they would be secure in the winter. Let us then hope that the olive may ere long be as much the emblem of Florida, as it has been of her mother country, from whose trammels she is at length freed.

While the olive trees are young and yet unbearing, the attention of the farmer will be directed to the *Benne* plant from which and from the poppy a fine table oil is procured nearly equalling that from the olive; it grows in almost any kind of soil ; the peculiar advantages of the benne and its history and productions, have been set forth at length in the publications upon Florida, which are already before the community and it is not necessary here to repeat them.

Oranges, lemons and limes are already in full bearing in many places, and their extensive introduction will one day supersede any imports from abroad : the plantain and banana will also in time prove lucrative to those who raise them. Preserves from the citron, shaddock, mango, pawpaw, tamarind, &c. may and ere long will be made in Florida equal to the most delicate kinds from the Antilles. The pine apple and the bread fruit will in the lower latitudes form elegant articles of culture, to be shipped to the northern cities, where they are always in request.

The fig is a native of the country, and the dried fruit is a profitable article of commerce.

The spices, gums, dye woods, and medicinal articles, may form the minor objects in the nursery, and fill up the time not employed in attending to those things which are cultivated in larger quantities.

The palma christi or castor oil is planted by many gentlemen in Georgia and South Carolina, who obtain from nine to twelve dollars per dozen bottles for the expressed oil ; the luxuriance with which this plant vegetates in Florida will cause it not to be neglected : it is an article of the materia medica, in much request, and perhaps but too little planted.

The dolichos or soy bean is said to produce in China, four crops annually : from this kidney bean is prepared the soy or Indian catsup. In the south of Spain and many parts of the Mediterranean this bean, or a variety of it, forms a large portion of the food of the lower class of people : it is there called *caravances* : as an article of subsistence for negro slaves this is nutritious, and apparently raised in the greatest abundance with facility.

Rice of course can readily be grown in the usual low situations ; but it is probable that all the lands fit for this grain, will be found to be more profitably devoted to the sugar cane.

A most important branch has yet to be treated of ; the breeding of the silk worm, which in this country is so easy : it would afford an employment to the children of the poor white settler who otherwise might be idle, useless, and contractive of indolent and bad habits : by introducing into every family the fashion of attending to these valuable insects, as much as to the poultry yard, the quantity of raw silk would be great enough, to form in no long time one of the staple commodities of Florida : this combined with the fruit cultures would complete the circle of small, quiet, domestic occupation, which is so desirable to form in every family that comes to reside in the territory. A remark on the best mode of rearing the mulberry trees on which the silk worms altogether subsist, may not be here improperly introduced.

The white mulberry is the best, and it should be sown by seed so as to spring up in the form of wide hedges of ten feet in breadth, leaving a lane between each : in this mode the leaves may very readily be gathered by a pair of sheers, or even by hand if it is thought proper to form the hedge of less width. The hand of taste will naturally place these hedges, so as to combine with the exterior fence of the garden; and take away the monotony of the uniform wooden palings, which usually enclose the flower plots or vegetable beds of our southern plantation gardens. Respecting the treatment of the worms and the methods used to reel off the silk, any Encyclopedia will explain them.

Hemp will flourish in this country : how far the introduction of it is eligible, is unknown, but it is thought that it might be profitable. There are a number of varieties of the palmetto, from whence the inhabitants and even the Indians form ropes : much of the small tackling of the fishing boats is made of this grass, which is rather the better for being kept wet, as it is apt to crack like rushes when dry : we also find in the country that palmetto, from whence the rigging, cordage and cables of most of the West India small craft are made.

The cork oak (quercus suber) being of quick growth might advantageously be planted, and would cause another foreign production to be dispensed with. The Spanish chesnut not only yields a harvest of ~~remarkable~~ *profitable* dry fruit, but by the elegance of its foliage and the depth of its shade would form a beautiful ornament to the grounds of a plantation.

Indian corn, buckwheat and guinea corn are among the most important bread stuffs, and constitute natural objects of cultivation : the latter grain is preferred by the West India negroes to the Indian corn, and is thought to be even more nutritive : it is also perhaps better adapted to the warm soil of Florida, producing most abundant returns : this as well as millet is peculiarly fit for fattening poultry. The sweet potatoe in its ~~three~~ *five* varieties need scarcely be mentioned, that and every esculent grows almost spontaneously and with a rapidity scarcely credible.

The dog grass of South Carolina or annual meadow grass has been recommended as the best adapted to be sown in Florida, where it succeeds in the very meanest soil. The clover and other foreign grasses probably require favorable spots, though the author has seen occasionally a few clover blades in the western pine lands, which indicate at least that they would live in soil not the richest. The scud or scots grass might also be tried.

14

Rye and oats succeed well and grow with great rapidity : as food for working horses the latter is certainly preferable even to the soft gold seed corn.

We have not yet made mention of the *tea plant* : that the latitude of Florida is sufficiently genial for its production there can be no doubt ; but whether the soil would answer, or if so whether it can be grown as cheap as the present importations from China, are questions that have not been considered. By obtaining the seeds in Canton and sowing them in tubs, young sprouts may with care and attention be safely brought over : the experiment is certainly worth trying, although many may sneer at the suggestion : but this was also the case when cotton was first tried, and will always attend what are considered innovations : it is to be hoped that there are in the union, men of enterprise who will not be easily discouraged from essaying : the profit if successful would amply repay : the trouble and disappointment would be small, and the expense not to be mentioned.

Remarks on the raising of stock do not come precisely under this head of the work, but as most other objects of the attention of the agriculturist have been treated of we may include all points relative to a nursery, farm or plantation.

Certainly one of the most eligible employs in Florida will be that of breeding large herds of cattle : the rains and dews create a luxuriant vegetation all the year, requiring only a regular and successive burning of the grass, to allow the young shoots to sprout : in other places mention has been made of the excellencies of the country for this object, and we can only repeat here the great advantages of the plan. Already the hides and tallow from South America are scarce, and it has been demonstrated by writers on political economy that the demand for leather in the world is greater than the annual supply and expedients are of course made : in the south the skin of the alligator is formed into water proof covering for the feet, and for saddle seats, and experiments are making to find other succedaneums. The cattle require no winter fodder ; the few wild animals will soon be extirpated and a single herdsman may attend to large droves.

Sheep may also be bred in numerous flocks : when the success of our manufactories have driven foreign broadcloths and woollen stuffs from the market, the demand for the fleeces will be great : the climate of Florida will tend to improve the texture of the wool and supplies of a superior quality will be sent to the northern marts.

The Angola goats may be brought into the country where they would find a temperature congenial to the one they inhabit, and the mohair would add another article to the long list of Florida productions.

The critical reader must not imagine that the discussion, of what are considered appropriate objects of agricultural attention, are merely Utopian : the country is capable of producing all, if the energies and skill of man are combined to attend to them : and can we doubt it ? Can we suppose that so many sources of wealth will remain unvisited, unexplored and rejected ? Certainly we must answer, No. The adoption of all will not come at once : each successful experiment will induce the trial of something new, until the resources of the country are fully developed, the territory thickly peopled and the tide of agriculture and commerce at the full.

It is doubtful whether a happier man will be found than a respectable independent planter, who fixed in a salubrious spot in Florida, finds on his farm every luxury that is so dearly purchased by the citizens of a crowded city : his sugar, tea, fruit, preserves, animal and vegetable food will be the produce of his own fields or farm yard : the rivers supply the most delicious shell and scale fish : the wild fowl are excellent and numerous : his vineyard, olive and orange groves will offer their unstinted products ; his orchards and his garden supply all to tempt and gratify the appetite : except for a few articles of wearing apparel, which if necessary could be supplied at home, he will be wholly independent of the world, while he will send out his cargoes of superfluous productions to supply the wants of his less fortunate fellow-citizens in more northern climes.   Such will be at a *future* day the situation of the Florida planter who *by a judicious arrangement of his capital and industry*, shall turn the silent forests into smiling fields and flourishing plantations.

OBSERVATIONS ON THE TEMPERATURE AND CLIMATE.

The climate of the whole of Florida during eight months of the year, from October to June, is delightful, and almost one continued spring; as the range of the thermometer in the hot months of summer is only from 84° to 88° of Fahrenheit, and constantly cooled by the sea breeze, they are by no means so oppressive as in Carolina or Georgia, and such intense sultry weather as marks the northern dog-days, is seldom if ever felt. On the Atlantic side the winds from the south and south-west make a thick heavy atmosphere, and impeding the airs from the ocean, cause an oppression and heat that create the only unpleasant sensations experienced during the Florida summer.

Generally speaking the springs and summers are dry, and the autumns changeable : the winters are mild and even serene ; snow is scarcely seen at St. Augustine twice in a century, but the black frost is an occasional visitant ; though at the severest times the ice has never been formed thicker than the sixteenth part of an inch ; its action has never extended south of cape Canaveral, and but very rarely reaches Mosquito inlet. The nipping of the white frost occasionally is felt so far as the extreme capes of Florida, though not an annual visitant. The duration of the frost or cold of any kind never lasts but a few hours, and seldom occurs more than once or twice in January, which is the severest month. The cold winds are always from the north-west.

In the peninsula of Florida rain is foretold one or two days before, either by an immoderate dew, or by the total absence of the dews on a calm night ; the winds from the north-east are cool and moist, and cause the frequent showers by which the sand of this climate is endued with a prodigious vegetative power : almost invariably when the rain has ceased, the sky does not continue overcast, but the clouds pass away, the horizon clears up, the sun again makes his appearance, and the breeze which brought the shower blows free and unsurcharged with moisture.

The rains and dews, without being troublesome, create at most seasons such a luxuriant vegetation, that the surface of the earth is never without good verdure. The long absence of the sun, the days and nights being nearly equal, gives the ground time to cool and recover from the daily evaporations.

Another pleasant consequence of this, is the very delightful freshness of the nights in the sultriest period of the year, by which the body is refreshed, the sleep sound, and the natural faculties restored to vigour.

As a precaution, a sheet of clean writing paper or a silk handkerchief placed in the hat keeps the head cool, when necessity requires an exposure to the summer sun : this is more needful, as light straw hats are generally worn.

Saint Augustine has always been healthy until the summer of 1821, when it was visited by the yellow fever which proved fatal to many strangers : we shall endeavour presently to account for this pestilence, and to show that its return is not to be dreaded, and that it is not an attendant either on this town or upon any part of Florida. No opportunity of information has been afforded respecting a similar scourge at Pensacola the last year, but that city having ever been free hitherto from such fatal fevers, similar causes to those in St. Augustine may have operated there.

That not only St. Augustine, but such parts of East Florida as have been occupied are healthy, is to be clearly inferred from the fact of the ninth regiment of British infantry having been stationed during the revolutionary war in detachments at St. Augustine, Matanzas, Picolati, and St. Marks on Apalachie, and during a period of twenty months not losing a single man by natural death.

That the climate is good for patients of a consumptive habit is notorious, several persons during the last winter and spring from Carolina and elsewhere having recovered their health ; and that the air is not at any season hurtful, is equally known from the circumstance of the native and foreign ladies walking till late in the moonlight on summer and autumn evenings, with only the slight coverings on their heads of their lace veils or *mantillas*, and many even without these. Medical men have stated that dampness or discolouring of plaister, soon moulding of bread, moistness of sponge, dissolution of loaf sugar, and rusting of metals, are marks of bad air : now all these are remarked in St. Augustine, and notwithstanding it is very healthy : this dampness is occasioned by the saline particles which arising from the sea, by no means occasion sicknesss.

And for the salubrity of West Florida we have the authority of Romans, who tells of an old man of eighty-three, who had very dutifully gone five miles on foot to catch fish for his *mother*, who had taken a fancy to a dish of that food, and in the meantime was busied at home in preparing a batch of bread.

The fashion of sending invalids from the north, on an expensive journey to the south of France and Italy, may perhaps be superseded, if the physicians could be induced to recommend a winter at St.

Augustine to their patients, who would thus, instead of being re-moved, perhaps to die in a foreign climate, be near their friends and within a few days' sail of their homes : admitting for one instant that the summer months are unhealthy, no one can doubt the salu-brity of the rest of the year.   The geniality of the climate, the beauty of the orange groves, the vicinity of the ocean, and the quie-tude of the place, would contribute greatly towards the restoration of health to consumptive persons.   Without entertaining any preju-dice in favour of St. Augustine, the attention of the faculty is seri-ously entreated by the author to this subject, and to the propriety of ordering their debilitated patients to try the salubrious air of Florida, which has in one remarkable instance restored a long crip-pled gentleman of New-York to the use of his limbs, a fact well known to all his acquaintance, who came in wonder to visit him on his return in full activity to New-York.

But although the sea coast, and the elevated lands in the interior are undoubtedly healthy, it is by no means certain that the banks of the large fresh water rivers are free from those miasmæ which generate intermittent fevers, agues, and the disorder known at the southward as *country fever :* in the fall of the year, when that sea-son is rainy, these complaints do occasionally appear, but they are confined to the immediate borders of the water courses, and do not extend to the high lands in the vicinity.   Upon the salt waters, such as Matanzas, Halifax, and Indian rivers, no such disorders exist, and hence the planters at Tomoco, Mosquito, &c. are perfectly free from sickness.

In proceeding to give a probable account of the rise of the yellow fever in St. Augustine, it must be prefaced by a sketch of the *local* situation of the town, in which brevity will be studied : the writer also begs leave to request that his theory may not be too fiercely assailed by gentlemen of the medical profession, who in the present era of discussion on so mysterious a subject, may differ as widely from the author as from each other : the conclusions attempted to be drawn from facts, appear natural ones, and are submitted for consideration in the study, not put forth as dogmas to the public.

The town of St. Augustine is situated on a neck of land, formed by the river Matanzas which is the harbour, on the east, and St. Sebastian's creek emptying thereinto, on the south and west ; on the north an entrenchment extends from the glacis of fort St. Mark, which is at the north end of the town upon the harbour, to the marshes of St. Sebastian's creek. This neck of land is divided into two peninsulas by a small stream called Mari-Sanchez creek, running parallel to the harbour, but heading in some low lands within the lines : it is on the eastern peninsula alone that the town is built, the western one being occupied by kitchen gardens, corn-fields, orange groves, and pasture grounds.

Somewhat more than half way between the fort and the south end of the western peninsula, a stone causeway and wooden bridge crosses Mari-Sanchez creek, and connects the two portions of the precincts of the town, and it is to the north of this causeway that the principal part of the buildings are placed, forming a parallelogram somewhat more than a quarter of a mile wide from east to west, and three quarters in length from north to south.

The houses on the side of the harbour are chiefly of stone, having only one story above the ground floor : these latter are invariably laid with a coat of *tabbia*, a mixture of sand and shells well known in our southern states, and are scarcely ever used but as store rooms, the families living in the upper story.

The dwellings with few exceptions, on the back streets, particularly in the north-west quarter, have but the ground floor ; and are generally built of wood, though stone ones are common, but almost all are laid with a tabbia flooring.

The undeviating salubrity of St. Augustine, while under the British flag, was certainly augmented by the perfect cleanliness and

15

neatness, which was the characteristic of the town during that epoch ; and that it continued so, while the buildings crumbled into ruins over the heads of the indolent Spaniards, and the dirt and nuisance augmented in every lot, is an additional proof of the natural healthiness of the place.

St. Augustine owed a large portion of its inhabitants to the many dependants on the Spanish government who held numerous small posts, the salaries of which were perhaps not punctually paid, but the daily allowance of rations in kind, enabled the holders to exist in their various shattered habitations which they were unable to repair, and in many instances only half occupied : and thus it was at the exchange of flags in July, 1821.

At this period, and for some time before and after, these families dependant on the government, and many others, emigrated to Cuba and left their houses and lots uncleaned and shut up ; the breaks in the dwellings however, open to the heavy rains which fell at that period, the waters of which of course stagnated where they fell.

The casemates of the fort had also many of the rooms disused and shut up, from a variety of causes, not the least of which were the leaks in the tabbia pavement of the platform.

The author lately heard it stated by a medical gentleman of high attainments, and now one of the first characters in Congress, who had honoured him with his friendship and acquaintance ; that a vessel whose hold was clean and empty, which should remain at anchor in any southern port during the hot summer months, would have the infectious miasmæ, which generates what is called yellow fever, collected in her hold, to which all going into it were exposed. Thus were endangered crowds of adventurers, mostly in a state of poverty, who flocked to St. Augustine and were pent in numbers in the common boarding houses that were opened in many of the tenements which had so long been closed.

The fever broke out in the back streets in isolated houses, and

each case was independent of the other : neither contagion nor infection were in any one case perceptible ; the foul air that generated disease was confined to each dwelling. Some of the most decided cases arose, when late in October there was hired for the occupation of the officers a house, that had been closed all the summer ;
it was in a close part of the town, but no sickness was near : three
or four of the officers fell almost immediate victims.

It is true that many died from the effects of inordinate indulgen-
cies, great exposure to the hot sun and heavy rains, and a few cases
could not be traced to satisfactory causes, but in general explanations could be given. Three or four vessels also came from the
Havana laden with fruit, which performed little or no quarantine ;
one had on her voyage lost the captain and all the crew ; and one lay
close along the wharf, aground at low water ; several cases were
clearly traceable to these vessels : but each nucleus of infection
does not appear to have expanded, nor was there any actual *infected
district*. The author and many of his friends were continually called on to visit and even nurse the sick, without having any appre-
hension of incurring any danger.

The humanity, the attention, and the friendly unremitted good
offices of the Spanish ladies, towards the sick strangers, will ever be
remembered with admiration by those who saw their efforts, and
with gratitude by those who experienced them. It is in woman's
bosom that all the virtues take a deeper root, and flourish as in a
more genial soil. The author has seen from these amiable females
a tenderness bestowed on the dying man, that would not have been
exceeded by the patient's own family, and the pillow of disease has
been propped, and the bed of death smoothed by the most maternal
and sisterly cares.

From what has preceded it is inferred that with a proper venti-
lation and a due attention to cleanliness and sobriety, St. Augustine
will never again be visited by so sweeping a pestilence, and we may

argue in proof thereof its remarkable salubrity this past year, not a single fatal case of fever having occurred in the space of the last fourteen months.

The very judicious arrangements which have been made lately, by the municipality of St. Augustine, will soon reproduce that perfect neatness and propriety, which formerly distinguished this town : its reputation for health established, we may hope that it will be a retreat in summer for the Carolinian and Georgian, and a shelter to the inhabitant of more northern states, from the rigor of their severe winters.

A society will thus be gradually formed, that may tempt the invalid to renew his visit annually, and induce many to join the colony which will be planted in the Montpelier of America.

OBSERVATIQNS UPON THE FLORIDA KEYS AND WRECKERS.

The general Florida reef commences at cape Florida, on the eastern coast in about latitude 25° 38′ N. and trends about southwest to bay Honda, twenty-five or thirty miles south of cape Sable, whence it sweeps nearly west until terminated by the Tortugas bank.

The edge of soundings, which are chiefly one hundred fathoms, are nearly parallel to the outer edge of the reef; within which, between the banks and the keys is a channel, where about fifteen feet may be carried all through : the general rule for sailing within the reef is, to have a careful man at the mast head to look out; from the transparency of the blue water he will see all the heads and shoals a good way off, in a clear day at least a mile, and thus making the eye the pilot, and keeping a middle channel, this dangerous navigation is passed.

Key Biscayne has been styled and is now called Cape Florida, though there is not actually any decided headland, and hence the uncertainty of the latitude : at the south end are wells : the inlet at the north end called *Bear Cut*, admits craft of six feet water into the bay behind where are the settlements : and the channel at the south the same.

Soldier's Key is six or seven miles to the southward, containing only a few roods of land.

ELLIOTT'S KEY next below, is eight miles in length and about half a mile wide : there is a harbor here with eight feet water, and an inlet over the reef of two fathoms nearly opposite : there is also an anchorage of ten feet under the lee of the island. Upon this key is a small quantity of land fit for vegetation and light productions.

Saunder's Cut, is to the north of *Elliott's key* and the inlet known as *Black Cæsar's creek* is to the south, dividing it from JENNING'S ISLAND a small spot, with two keys at its south end forming an inlet known by the name of *Angel-fish creek.* Here commences the long irregular land called KEY LARGO, about the middle of which is the promontory of *Sound point.*

Sound point, is the only spot that may be said to form a true promontory, from the Rocky springs a little south of Jupiter inlet. This point has sometimes been named cape Florida, but the Spaniards having designated the southern end of key Biscayne by that name, their appellation has prevailed. It is on *Sound point,* that is on the extensive reef before it, that almost every vessel that is cast away meets her fate. The north point of that reef (*Carysfort*) extends as far as *Angel-fish creek* and its south point which is dry, marks a deep channel to go in towards *Key Tavernier.* The people who watch the misfortunes of navigators, to make a benefit of them (the wreckers) know so well how much ships are exposed in approaching this reef, that they station themselves a little south of the point, from whence they can with certainty wait for the sight of any ship, that is so unfortunate as to be driven ashore : hence *Key Tavernier* has become for the last fifty years the general rendezvous of the little fleet of small craft, which are annually fitted out for wrecking, of which more notice will be taken presently

Cayo Largo, Long key or *Sound point key*, is actually a peninsula. In 1769 captain Bernard Romans with great labor, fatigue, inconvenience from musquitos, and a total want of fresh water for four or five days, explored its inside waters. He was stimulated to this enterprise by the reports of the Providence and Spanish fishermen, who told him unanimously, that they had often tried to enter at *Angel-fish creek* and to come out at *Boca Herrera*, the creek oppposite to *key Tavernier*; or the contrary way, but always in vain, nor did any of them know an instance of its having been done. Captain Romans then went in at *Angel-fish creek*, and after a great deal of time spent in Sandwich gulf, no passage was found : he afterwards entered into Grant's lake, by drawing the boat over dry ground for above six times her own length. Out of this lake he found his way, by a very narrow passage at the south end : but as no part of *key Largo* yields any fresh water, and after he got into Grant's lake all the ground round him being mangrove swamp, he was unable to find any : two of his people were nearly exhausted by thirst, which it was impossible to alleviate till he reached the watering place at *Matacombe*. This is stated by way of caution if any stranger should get there : for though he will find abundance of fresh water on every other part of the coast, he ought not to venture to be for any purpose, within this peninsula of *key Largo*, without a store of that invaluable necessary.

Key Largo formerly abounded with mastic, lignum vitæ and mahogany, but the most valuable has been long cut down, and there is none now but very young timber. A portion of good rich land is on this key, among the principal growth of which is found the wild cinna·mon, wild olive, &c. : in most places where capable of cultivation, the soil is a rich black mould of considerable depth : the larger growth heavy, but the under brush not so thick as usual in the ordinary hammocks. *Key Largo* has no living animals on it except racoons and insects. The south end of *key Largo* is determined by a small creek scarce a musquet shot wide, admitting only boats and called by the Spaniards *Boca Herrera.* The bay within abounds with fish, turtle, and lobsters.

KEY TAVERNIER has little or no high ground, affording only sand crabs and some few doves and other birds. There is here a small harbor within a reef where the wreckers usually lie. Nearly east from this key lies the southern point of *Carysfort reef* making a wide channel called *Palmeston in and outlet :* this south point is dry, but in the channel is four and five fathoms, and ships in distress may find shelter under the point.

From *key Largo* passing by *Bull's island* with a little key at its south end, the navigator proceeds to YOUNG MATACOMBE, which is four miles long with a well of good fresh water at the east end : abreast of this key is a clump of sunken rocks called the *Hen and Chickens.*

Next to the south west is the island of OLD MATICOMBE remarkable for being the most convenient and the best watering place on all this coast : on its east end are *five* wells in the solid rock, said to have been cut by the Indians, but which appear to be natural chasms, similar to those found on many parts of the peninsula of Florida : they yield excellent water in abundance as do likewise some ponds near them. This island was one of the last habitations of the Indians of the *Coloosa* nation. There are some good rich lands upon it capable of cultivation. About a mile towards its north east end lies a small bushy gravelly key, on the extremity of a reef : it is called *Matanza,* that is *slaughter,* from the catastrophe of a French crew, said to have amounted to near three hundred men, who were unfortunate enough to fall into the hands of the *Coloosas,* by whom they were to a man murdered on this spot. *Matanza key* is the leading mark for finding the watering place on *Matacombe,* in the channel to which is ten feet water.

East from *old Matacombe* is the south point of *Matanza reef* and *Spencer in and outlet :* from which the *Great reef* begins to be divided into smaller spots; the channel within them is likewise deeper and wider, but there is less smooth water than from key *Biscayne* to key *Tavernier*.

Key Vivora is the next key, beyond which is *Cayos Vacas* or *Cow keys*, on the largest and westernmost of which is tolerable water plenty of deer.

The next islands are called BAY HONDA KEYS, extending some leagues westwardly. Beyond these is *Newfound Harbor*, due south from which, and four miles off is *key Looe*, a little sandy bar or island which takes its name from the British ship of war *Looe* having been lost there. To the east of *key Looe* is *Dartmouth in and outlet*, through which all vessels generally pass that go from St. Augustine to the Havana. A few miles further westward is the island called by the Spaniards CAYO HUESSO (*Bone key*) and by the English KEY WEST; since the cession of the Floridas to the United States it has received the name of THOMPSON'S ISLAND.—It extends east and west for six or seven miles, having a shallow bank before it : at the north-east end is a small anchorage ground called *Spanish Harbor* ; the principal harbor or roadstead is at the west end; but it is considered unsafe in northern and western gales. There is about twenty-four feet water, and the way in is to keep close on board the west side of the small key which lies some miles to the south-east of the west point of THOMPSON'S ISLAND : draw close enough alongside this key to chuck a biscuit on shore : then steer about N. W. by N. to the point of the island.

Key West is perhaps two miles across in the very widest place ; and is naturally divided into two parts differing materially from each other : the west end offers a considerable body of rich dark mould interspersed with loose limestones ; the timber growing on it is neither high nor large, but the underbrush is very thick : at this end fresh water is found in abundance and of good quality. The eastern half has very little good soil upon it : the salt ponds of which so much

16

has been spoken, extend nearly all through it; they are separated from each other and from the inlets and bays formed by the sea, by solid rocks and loose stones almost destitute of vegetation. The water in them, as they now are in a state of nature, is about two feet deep pretty uniformly, and extremely salt: the ponds are generally allowed to be of the very best kind, and of an extent sufficient when properly attended, to supply the United States; it is singular that no other of the Florida keys contain such natural ponds, though possibly artificial ones might be constructed on them in favorable situations.

Deer are extremely abundant, as well as a variety of birds: indeed almost all the adjacent keys are well supplied in this respect, if they yield fresh water. The tide ebbs and flows here regularly six feet, and the time of high water at the full and change is eight o'clock. The Havana bears from hence S. 6 degrees, W. twenty-five leagues, but vessels steer higher up on account of the currents.

Key West was granted to Don Juan P. Salas, the private secretary to governor Coppinger of East Florida, but it is at present claimed by general John Geddes of Charleston, S. C. and by Mr. Symington, both of whom have establishments upon the island, and are both in possession. The title of the former gentlemen has been pronounced by the attorney general of the United States as clear and indisputable: Mr. Symington has also obtained some first rate legal opinions decidedly in his favor.

At *key West* terminates what was formerly called by the British *Hawke channel*, but which is now known as the passage through the keys; from this passage there are several channels into the Gulf of Mexico: the first of these passages is to the west end of *old Matacombe island*, but will admit no vessel of above six feet draught of water: it is called *Onslow passage*, passing near Cayo Axi or Sandy key, off cape Sable: the second passage is at the south west end of *Vivora island* with nine feet water: the third or *Gordon's passage* has eight and a half feet water : the fourth has the name of *North passage* : it opens at the west end of the southernmost of the *bay Honda keys*, and goes along the north east side of the largest of the *Martyrs* : its depth of water is seven feet, but it is narrow and difficult. None of these passages are now much in use, except by the fishermen and turtlers.

The fifth passage called by the Spaniards *Boca Chica*, lies between *key West* and *Mule keys*: vessels from the southward in the stream should stand in through key West channel or in coming down through the keys ; after clearing the south point of KEY WEST, steer in, keeping close on board the shore within thirty or forty yards, then laying N. N. W. until all shoals are cleared ; the lowest soundings are fourteen feet. To the westward of key West channel are two others, one between *Mule key* and *Marquis bank*, called *Boca Grande :* the other lies between that bank and the *dry Tortugas shoals* and is the westernmost and broadest of all.

The *Martyr keys* lying back between *bay Honda* and *key West* may be divided into two classes : the high, and the low or drowned islands. The high islands are based upon grey, white or black hard rocks ; the low or mangrove islands are founded on coral rocks, covered with a rich but wet soil. The high islands are heaped in places with sand on which little or nothing grows : in other parts they have a stratum of bluish marl, on which flourish in great abundance and in a most agreeable temperature, a large variety of tropical trees, shrubs and plants. None of the islands are inhabited. The quantity of fish, and loggerhead, hawsbill and green turtle found here is almost incredible, particularly about *bay Honda :* among the long catalogue of fishes is a remarkable species of prawn which in a former page has been improperly noticed as a lobster : it wants in fact the two claws : it is found, sometimes weighing several pounds, in the holes of the coral rocks, beautifully spotted with red, yellow, blue, green, grey, and a little black, but all change into one red color in boiling : the ~~other~~ *various* fish are excellent in their kind, and may like all other fish caught on the Florida shore, be eaten with safety, which is not the case always in the Bahamas. From the promontory of *key Largo* the chain of the Florida keys on the south, and the coast of the main down to cape Sable on the north, *form* ~~from~~ what was formerly called *Richmond bay*: this is very shallow and full of grass and mud banks : and a labyrinth of small keys intervene behind the principal ones already described from the *Martyr's* to *key Largo*.

The MARQUIS BANK and KEYS and the MULE KEYS extend for a long distance westwardly from *Thompson's island*, having no reef in front. Hence to the DRY TORTUGAS BANK AND KEYS is twelve leagues terminating the general Florida reef.

It has more than once been a matter of discussion respecting the most eligible places for naval and military stations on the keys ; from all the information that has been collected, it would seem that *key West* or *Thompson's island* is the best as a naval *depot*, but probably vessels of small draught might advantageously be placed at *old Matacombe*, or *key Tavernier*, as cruisers : at *Matacombe* a military post might be established equally advantageously as at *cape Florida* or *key West*, and it would be mid-way between both : an establishment for the purposes to be mentioned presently might also be made at *Matacombe*, which besides its central situation and fine water, has a proportion of good land fit for agricultural or at least horticultural purposes. It would scarcely be worth the expense or trouble to erect permanent forts at any of these places, and a due consideration of the purposes required to be effected by military and naval posts, will quickly determine which of the three is the most eligible.

In the event of a war, various stations for cruizers would be appointed along the extensive general reef, where every vessel bound northward might be watched : the abundance of fish, turtle, and game in and among the keys would prove a constant source of refreshment : ~~from~~ hence also the pirates might be watched, when driven from their haunts and hiding places in the various obscure *keys* ~~haunts~~ around the island of Cuba and the Bahama banks.

The wreckers have been more than once mentioned and a slight notice of these people may not be unacceptable. For many years *wrecking* has beeen reduced to a perfect system, and upon the coast of Florida has been engrossed by the inhabitants of the Bahama islands, and principally by those of the island of New-Providence. The usual custom in fitting out these small craft on a wrecking and turtling voyage (for they are generally combined) is upon shares : the merchants of Nassau are chiefly the proprietors of the vessels, into which a few barrels of pork and buscuit are put, the crews being supposed able to subsist themselves by fishing and hunting, and these crews are composed of the pilots and fishermen of the islands.

Forty or fifty wreckers have often made their rendezvous at *Key Tavernier*, which has before been noted as a central position for their purposes, and at these times one or two vessels have been selected to fish for the others, in which case they always had a share of any booty.

On returning to Nassau, the government duties, admiralty fees, the tythe to the resident governor, and a variety of other colonial charges, took on an average thirty-five per cent., from the gross amount of the sales of the property brought in by the wreckers : one moiety of the nett proceeds then fell to the owner and fitter out of the craft ; the other half was divided among the captain and crew in certain shares and portions of shares, as agreed upon previous to the commencement of the expedition.

It has been estimated that the duties to the British government alone produced an annual revenue of fifteen thousand pounds sterling from this curious source ; besides keeping a numerous body of hardy and enterprising subjects in employ, and repaying with great profit the speculations of the merchants. It is also a notorious fact that since the termination of the late war, the town of Nassau has been almost supported by the wreckers, who are so sensible of the advantages derived from their employment, that they have openly declared they will never leave the reef, until driven off by armed force, and seem to consider themselves possessed of a right in the *wrecking ground* as their own individual property, independent of any change of government.

The great effect of gales of wind upon the Florida or gulf stream, the uncertainty of the line of the *eddy*, and the numerous baffling currents continually drive the mariner upon the reefs : the unexperienced navigator too is sometimes by light winds and unknown *sets* of the gulf accidentally carried within side the reef, through some of the inlets, and when he has got out an anchor, he sees through the clear water, that he is surrounded by rocks and shoals, which are more appalling to the eye than dangerous in reality, often lying in deep places. It is then that the wrecker makes his appearance, and the frightened master of a rich laden vessel, is compelled to accede to the terms of the only pilots who can take him safely out, for which in many instances two and three thousand dollars have been paid : there is seldom any competition, for by a point of honour among them no wrecker interferes with the one who first finds the bewildered vessel.

The variety of the modes of gain, and the different kinds of imposition, smuggling, &c. would fill a volume ; but on the other hand by trusting too much to the captain of the rescued vessel, it has more than once occurred that he has given bills of exchange which have never been paid, and made engagements and promises, which unless fulfilled before the extrication of his vessel, have been broken without a scruple when he found himself once more safe in the open sea.

In justice to the wreckers among the Florida keys, it must be remarked that much of the abuse which has been thrown upon them is very undeserved, and that where in one instance they are accused of extortion, there are many more where they have been ill treated for their services.

The idle tales which have been told of their making false lights on the coast, all who have resided in those parts, assure to be untruths. Those fires are occasioned by the hunters and Indians who burn the forests to clear them of underbrush, and to procure fresh pasture for the deer. Lightning also often sets fire to trees, and it is not very uncommon, in dry seasons, to see spontaneous flames arise in marshy places. But after all, what business has a mariner who knows there are no harbours or light-houses on this coast, to follow a light out of his course? and would it not be adviseable for any one passing along this coast, upon seeing a light to the westward, to look out for breakers if he stands in for that quarter?

We understand that lately a considerable number of small craft, have been sent down from various Atlantic ports upon voyages of wrecking and turtling, but they should be protected in some mode by the American government, and measures taken to prevent the interference of foreigners with their lawful pursuits.

An establishment at *Old Matacombe* would be very convenient, where some authorised persons could reside to regulate by rule and law, to determine upon the rates of pilotage in extreme cases, and prevent imposition on the one hand and the want of a sufficient remuneration on the other. A revenue vessel of light draught of water would be a preventive to many disorders and keep off the Providence wreckers, who might shun an armed cutter when they would laugh at any regulations that were not supported by competent strength, and put into effect by force of arms.

Sources of considerable profit in various respects are to be found upon the Florida reef, and among the archipelago of keys: the quantity of wrecked property annually thrown here is very great, and can only be fully known to those who have long been in the habit of wrecking: the number of vessels fitted out from Nassau is the greatest proof. Turtle shell and drift logwood and mahogany are no small branches of emolument ; the quantity of turtle taken is vast : a gentleman in Nassau has amassed a very large fortune lately by purchasing all the turtle not wanted for the consumption of the Bahamas, with which he makes very large quantities of turtle soup : this after being boiled to a hard jelly is preserved in cases perfectly air tight and sent to London, by which the soup in that city can be afforded to be sold at nearly one half the former prices. Would not a similar supply be acceptable to our northern cities ?

No attempt has been made by the author to introduce any sailing directions through this intricate navigation : he refers the navigator to the gulf pilot by captain Bernard Romans, De Brahm, &c. from which many of the preceding observations have been abstracted, and which contain minute directions ; the eye is however chiefly recommended, the clearness of the water shewing all dangers.

In closing the remarks upon the Florida keys, it is with satisfaction we find that a minute exploration of them is about to take place under the orders of the general government, and we may shortly expect to find many facts brought to light and many errors corrected : we may hope that the minuteness and accuracy of the new charts may enable the navigator to avoid many of the dangers, and that a familiarity with the passages, may teach him to pass this long dreaded coast in comparative safety.

When a few years shall have induced a trade from the harbours on the western coast of the Florida peninsula, a knowledge of the passes through the keys into the gulf of Mexico will be requisite for the shipmaster to shorten his voyage, and it is not impossible but an intimate knowledge of the navigation may lead to the laying down of some rules for the hitherto dubious courses through the reef.

OBSERVATIONS UPON THE INDIANS.

———————

The Indians were formerly very numerous in the Floridas, per-haps as much so as in Mexico : the histories of Ferdinand de Soto and other early travellers assure us of this fact, and the vestiges that remain to the present day attest it. From various causes how-ever, they have gradually, and within the last forty years rapidly disappeared, particularly from East Florida ; and the numerous tribes are reduced to some small bands and a few ruinous villages of indolent dirty vagabonds, wholly unlike the bold character of American Indians.

The Floridas having almost constantly belonged to Spain, their mode of considering the rights of the Indians is perhaps the one to be referred to, when that question shall be agitated : and this, be-cause their relations with the aborigines of America have been very different to those of most other nations.

Having obtained a grant from his holiness the pope, " he who kept the keys of heaven," to all those parts of the western hemis-phere they should discover, they made a lodgment on a spot of a province or kingdom, and having fortified it, entered into treaties

17

of incorporation with the nearest tribes, and thus gradually advanced to those more remote. Cortez varied in Mexico a part of this mode of process, but not the principle : he went straight to the capital, but after becoming firmly footed there, carried on the system of incorporation.

The pope made those grants in order to extend the Catholic religion, founded no doubt on the credence of those days in his boundless powers, and on the immensity of good in the object ; and perhaps these were as good data of primitive territorial rights, as those of most other nations : he gave what was not his, and others have taken what was not theirs.

However this incorporating system may have been abused in practice, as very many of the intentions of all governments are, when acted upon far from home, it must be allowed that it intimately combined benevolence in its leading principles ; that in practice, it exhibited a perpetual reciprocity of interests, and that the depopulation of the aborigines under this system, has been much less rapid than in other parts, even where the purchasing system has been preferred. In New Spain but a small defalcation comparatively exists of the Indians, and that may be traced to the amalgamation with the whites ; but where alas ! are the tribes that once inhabited the territory between the Floridas and the St. Lawrence ? We refer here only to the Spanish *continental* settlements, for on the *islands* it would appear that extermination had been the order of the day, and that the after plans of incorporation had grown out of the horrors of those.

People of all countries from a remarkable effect of habit, are prone to suppose their method of managing, to be the best and only means by which a desired end can be effected. This doubtless induced the British government to discontinue the Spanish system of incorporation, upon their obtaining possession of Florida at the peace of 1763 ; for soon after, treaties were held with the Indians.

and a line of demarcation was established ; pointing out decidedly the lands of the white and red nations respectively : according to the words of the treaty the British government retained the lands, " all round the sea shore back as far as the tide rises ; all the lands on the east side of the river St. John, from its source until it runs into the sea ; all the lands to the westward of the river St. John, that are situated between the sea and a line drawn from the place where the Ocklawaha creek falls into the said river, near Spalding's old upper trading house, to the forks of the Black creek at Colwill's plantation, and from thence to that part of the river St. Mary which is intersected by a continuation of the line to the entrance of Turkey creek into the Alatamaha ;" which place upon the river St. Mary is at or near Coleraine in Georgia.

The existence of this line, which was actually marked through the woods, has been doubted, but the evidence of its having been fixed remains in the records of East Florida : the older Indians have a distinct idea of it, and the author has heard them allude to it, and they are under the strong impression that it is by that line of demarcation their lands are now to be meted. This treaty was made in 1769 by governor Tonyn.

In 1784 we learn that the Spanish government of East and West Florida, met the Talahassy and Seminole Indians in a body, who held those districts with their celebrated warrior McGillivray at their head, and formed and executed a treaty of incorporation, (or rather reformed and re-executed the treaty which the British occupancy and treaty had rendered obsolete) which completely made the Indians of Spain coequal with the whites, and put the sovereignty into the hands of his catholic majesty. That treaty stipulates that the sovereignty, rights and jurisdiction of his majesty, go alike through all parts of these provinces. And this the United States virtually acknowledged in treating with Spain, and Spain only, on the boundary line between the Floridas and Georgia, and which line was moreover run under a military force, expressly to guard against interference on the part of the Indians. The same treaty says, that should the Indians be dispossessed of their lands (for they had a right to lands individually but none nationally) his majesty will remunerate them in other parts of his territory. Each Indian had a right to land, as well as and on the same footing with white, free black and coloured subjects, in any part of the province.

However this might have been understood by the Spanish government, the Indians themselves have always entertained the idea that their boundaries remained as fixed by the British, and their opposition to, and final stoppage of the running of the Florida line, demonstrates this, as well as their hostility to any whites who crossed the line. It is a matter of notoriety that no Spaniard, previous to the exchange of flags, dared to cross the river St. John above Buena Vista, and the Spanish governors in their talks from time to time, seem to have tacitly consented to this assumption of the Indians.

The history of a purchase made from the Indians, under permission from and ratified by the Spanish government, proves on the other hand that the Indians could not make sales without their sanction, and goes far towards the inference that it should rather be considered as a grant from Spain.

The house of Panton, Leslie & Co. stands identified with the history of the Florida Indians. Spain having received back the Floridas from Great Britain, neglected no step to assuage the regret of the red people, at parting with their friends the British, and to conciliate their good will. In the earliest meeting, the Indians requested to be supplied with English goods and by English merchants ; and having been desired by the government, to point out the commercial house most to their satisfaction, among the many with whom they had traded, they chose that of Panton, Leslie & Co. This advantage gained and carefully improved by the principals of that house, men of the first rate talents, information and address, it soon became the monitor of the Indians, the guardian of the tranquillity of the province, and a favorite with the court of Spain. They had several trading establishments in each province, and were allowed to import articles of commerce of every description free of duties, when foreign goods were so strictly forbidden, that to be detected introducing a single piece of linen, would have subjected by the laws of Spain, any other persons, to the penalty of working in the mines for life. They became the sole suppliers of all articles wanted by the government, garrisons, inhabitants and Indians of East and West Florida.

During this lucrative range of political and civil importance, the firm had credited generally and largely the Indians of both provinces, at that time a numerous body : for tribes, afterwards shut into Georgia, then traded to their stores ; and preferring, as a matter of accommodation to all concerned to receive a body of land, as a general extinction of those debts, rather than urge individual payments, they obtained permission from the Spanish court to treat with the Indians on that head. A total extinction of debts so easily obtained, was of course pleasing to the Indians, and not injurious to Spain, who held lands only to give to those in whose possession they might become nationally beneficial ; a treaty was concluded between that house and their debtors, and Spain *ratified* the treaty ; thereby virtually ceding to the house of Panton, Leslie & Co. a territory of about twelve hundred thousand acres for the purposes of discharging the debts of her Indian subjects. These lands which descended to the firm of John Forbes & Co. of Matanzas in the island of Cuba as the surviving partners of the house of Panton, Leslie & Co. are situated between the Appalachie and Appalachicola rivers, and are generally known as *Forbes' purchase.*

So much would not have been stated on this subject, did it not involve a curious and important question relative to Florida lands and grants : if the line of demarcation laid down by the British, was conclusive against the Spanish government and recognised by them, all the grants made by the governors, within the Indian territory, and they constitute a large portion of the whole, may be considered as *ab initio* void, and the United States may be compelled to obtain the Indian lands, within this line, by treaty and purchase : and on the other hand, should the principle of the Spanish sovereignty over the whole country be adopted, it will naturally follow that all the *bonā fide* grants made within the Indian territory are binding on the United States, who are likewise bound to protect and provide other lands for their Indian subjects, should those they occupy be wanted.

The Indians of East Florida are supposed not to exceed one thousand souls ; or upon the widest calculation fifteen hundred : they consist generally of tribes of the Seminole nation, but there are among them many refugees from the Creeks, Choctwas, Alabamas, and other hostile tribes, the scattered remnants of those who in 1818 broke up the Seminole settlements. The first disorganization of the Florida Indians arose, upon the breaking up and retirement of the trading houses of Panton, Leslie & Co. : then came the irruption of the Georgia borderers in 1812, when the Alachua settlements were destroyed, and their king and chief, *Payne,* received his death wound in the field : his brother *Bowlegs* died soon after of a broken heart and the Indians remaining without a chief of talent or enterprise, order was lost among them : their defeats in 1818 completely broke them up, and they are now dispersed in small squads and single families all over the country : a few still inhabit the small villages between Alachua and Tampa bay ; mingled with parties of their foes many have come to the waters on the eastern side of the peninsula ; and others emaciated and naked supply wood to the city of St. Augustine, carried in bundles on their backs. Among the wanderers are a family of the Euchee nation. The whole of them will no doubt submit to any system that will ameliorate their life which at present is very wretched : they are humbled to the dust. The author was last year a witness to the most absolute state of starvation they were reduced to, from the loss of their crops in 1821 ; at the period when the attention of themselves and their negro slaves were directed to the cultivation of their crops, a few worthless wretches from St. Augustine, for the purpose of alarming the Indians, and inducing them to sell their slaves for almost nothing, a practice of imposition that had often before been practiced, went into the nation and spread reports that two thousand American troops under the command of General Jackson were coming down to expel them from their lands and carry away their slaves and cattle. The Indians upon this abandoned their crops and sold many of their slaves, by which the avarice of the speculators was gratified. It has been reported that a similar experiment was about to have been tried the last summer, but fortunately it miscarried in its birth.

Many of the emigrant Creeks and others who had got down to Tampa bay, and its waters launched their canoes there, and tempted by the smoothness of the summer ocean, ventured along the coast as far as cape Sable, when they became acquainted with the Bahama wreckers, who employed them to hunt on the cape and adjacent keys, in return for bread stuffs and trifling presents ; the game beginning to grow scarce, the wreckers carried a few of them through the reef to the woods immediately west of cape Florida ; large bodies soon followed and these refugees quickly spread along the east coast as far north as Jupiter inlet.

The remnant of the black and colored people who had served with colonel Nichols during the late war, fugitive slaves from all the southern section of the union, as well as from the Spanish plantations in Florida and from St. Augustine followed upon the steps of the Indians, and formed considerable settlements on the waters of Tampa bay. When the Indians went in pursuit of these negroes, such as escaped made their way down to cape Florida and the reef, about which they were collected within a year and a half past to upwards of three hundred : vast numbers of them have been at different times since carried off by the Bahama wreckers to Nassau, but the British authorities, having invariably refused to allow them to be landed, they have been smuggled into the remoter islands, and at this period, large numbers have been found on St. Andrews and the Biminis.

The chiefs of the outcast Indians who had by means of the wreckers found a mode of communicating with the governor of Nassau, once or twice went over, but were coolly treated. On the last visit they were imprisoned for a while, and then sent back without presents, and the shipmasters forbidden under heavy penalties to bring them over again. For several years past they have been very troublesome on the coast, plundering the wrecks and destroying the game, and at cape Florida have been made the instruments in the hands of one designing individual, of oppressing the very few settlers on that point. At the present time the greater portion of these Indians are about Charlotte harbour ; not more than fifty were on the east coast lately, and were preparing to join their countrymen, on the conclusion of the hunting season. No greater proof need be adduced of the impassable state of the country, than the fact of these Indians communicating with Charlotte harbour by coasting round the peninsula, instead of striking directly across, a course which they all unite in stating they have attempted from both sides in vain, being always stopped by the waters of the Never Glade.

Whatever steps the United States government may adopt respecting the Indians, they will doubtless be founded on principles of justice and humanity ; and their efforts will be directed to their improvement and civilization. On this head the author must quote the words of George I. F. Clarke, Esq. of Florida, to whom he is chiefly indebted for the materials of the preceding part of this article.

" The hand of aid and instruction properly extended, will make the Indians serviceable ; they will learn to labor, and our good example will wear out their former propensities. I know that there are some who will smile with contempt at the idea of taming Indians ; but I trust that their number and influence are very small. How limited must be the conception, how illiberal the mind to the contrary ! how little or how partially must they have studied human nature ! Are we not all the children of habit, the mere reflections of education and manners ? and why should these be incorrigible ? It is evident, that the only difference in man, laying aside his color, is the difference of opinion ; and that difference of opinion arises from the difference of education. Let the sceptical in this part of the philosophy of human nature turn his eyes to the city of Mexico, and see there the examples of talents natural and acquired, in the fine arts and belles lettres, manifest among Indians ; let him look into the Havana and see the many finished workmen in the useful and elegant crafts, to be found there among the Africans ; let him view man in all parts of the world, where he has had opportunities for his improvement, no matter where born or by whom begot and then let him declare if he is not always the master-piece of Nature's works and the only master of arts. And after thus seeing what he has acquired, will the caviller attempt to say what bounds have been prescribed to his acquirements by his country or his color ?"

OBSERVATIONS UPON THE LAND TITLES.

The lands which have been granted in both Floridas, under the administration of Great Britain and Spain, are not in their gross amount very considerable, with the exception of the few large concessions. The questions that are likely to arise upon them, will not probably involve the point of validity except in certain cases, but will turn on the location ; as much of the valuable ground is covered by conflicting grants : this will particularly be the case should the old British concessions be admitted to proof, for the lands taken up by them being in general of fine quality, were petitioned for by and allotted to Spanish subjects, and many of the grants for services are located upon these grounds.

When Great Britain withdrew from Florida, all her subjects who left the country were renumerated for their lands, excepting it is believed, those who remained in the United States or in the Floridas, and the claimants under these circumstances alone can pretend to set up a title.

Towards the close of the existence of the Spanish government in the Floridas, and perhaps for ten years previous to the signing of the treaty, the inhabitants foresaw that these provinces must unevitably become an integral part of the United States : They could not but perceive that strangers to their habits, manners, customs and religion would ere long rule the country ; and did they not possess some inherent right in the soil, they judged, and not without reason, that they might be lost in the current of the new population. Their lands therefore were to become an indispensible property, and unconnected with a government which then supported them, they must obtain tracts either to dispose of at an advantageous opportunity, or for the purpose of bending themselves to the labors of agriculture. With this prospect, all those entitled to them solicited grants for services, and obtained them by virtue of certain special ordinances from the court of Spain. It was their right so to do, and their motive was assuredly praiseworthy and justifiable : they were prompted by the same sacred instigation that induces the actions of all mankind, in making a provision for their offspring.

Hence the number of concessions made in the latter years of the government of Spain in Florida, compared with those of the earlier periods : but the circumstance of the 24th of January, 1818, having been fixed upon by the treaty as the date, posterior to which no grant is to be recognized by the American government, will if strictly enforced, cut off a large number of meritorious concessions, which were issued as a reward for services, by virtue of the royal orders before mentioned, particularly the one dated in 1815. The effect of these orders being to remunerate citizens for beneficial acts done to the government, it would seem almost proper to infer that all, who might thenceafter make out their right of reward and the previous non-remuneration, had an inchoate title created to their respective quotas from the very date of the order, although they happened to apply for them after a certain day which was not finally determined on until twelve months from it had elapsed : hence two equally deserving individuals having applied for their several bounties, earned painfully

by their blood and toil, on the 23d and 25th of January, 1818, respectively ; the one would have a good title, and the other be excluded
by the treaty and be deprived of his reward.   There was no time
fixed for the inhabitants to come in and claim their concessions, and
many delayed from that assurance, and from a want of means to pay
the fees upon their preliminary titles.

Upon the subject of the date of the 24th of January, 1818, extensive legal opinions from American and Spanish jurists have been given, which go the length to state, that by the constitution of Spain ;
(which was promulgated at Cadiz on the 19th March, 1812, and after a bloodless revolution was on the 7th March, 1820, adopted as it
was originally made, and then sworn to by Ferdinand the seventh)
the king had not the power to do any act, which took away property
from a Spanish subject ; and the eighth article of the treaty *which
did so*, by the act of fixing the date, was not confirmed by the Cortes,
but only the second and third articles, which transferred the sovereignty and the public lands to the United States.

As we are not lawyers we quit this subject, having ventured upon
it but for a moment, to plead something on behalf of those Floridians
whose titles are destroyed by the treaty, without any fault alleged
or implied of their own.

The investigation of the various intricate claims in Upper and
Lower Louisania, have brought to light a variety of the usages of
the Spanish government, respecting the mode of granting and taking
up lands ; and from the statements made in Congress, and more particularly the learned elucidation afforded by Messrs. Barton and Ben-
son, much of the mystery thrown around them has been cleared up.

It is now admitted, that the fact of an actual survey or location, is
by no means to be assumed as any criterion of the validity of a claim :
it would be a rule indiscrimiate in its character, and not distinguish-
ing between valid and invalid concessions.   If a concession be good
or bad, it is so from causes and facts anterior to the fact of survey or

location, and wholly independent of it ; it is so from causes co-eval or co-existent with the issuing of the concession or warrant itself ; it is either good or bad *then*, and the subsequent location or survey happening sometime after, and dependant on circumstances of personal convenience or personal influence, is wholly immaterial to the intrinsic merits of the concession.

In fuller corroboration of this fact it must be mentioned, that in Florida when the unconditional grants for civil or military services were made, the petitioner often named a place which was specially stated in the grant ; but when upon examination, the spot he had chosen was found to have been already taken up, he was allowed to locate elsewhere, and the survey and plat returned accordingly ; upon the well recognized principle that the grant, being made without prejudice to a third person, held good against the government when once issued, to be located elsewhere, when the specified spot was occupied.

Among the various modes in which lands are occupied in Florida, some are by grants from the crown of Spain direct : others from the governor general of Cuba, but the most from the colonial governors : some are held by a written permission for certain purposes, such as erecting mills or bridges ; and in some instances land is occupied, the original tenure to which was from the verbal permission of the governor. This practice was always countenanced by the Spanish government, in order that poor persons when they found themselves a little at their ease, might at their own conveniency apply for and obtain complete titles : in the meantime such imperfect rights were suffered by the government to descend by inheritance, and even to be transferred by private contract : when requisite they have been seized by judicial authority, and sold for the payment of debts.

In making the grants for services it was not contemplated either by the authorities or by the individuals, that these lands were to be actually occupied : most of the grantees were in some capacity or other holders of offices under the government, and resided in St. Augustine, and wished to continue there : the Spaniard is different from the American in all his habits, and more particularly as a settler ; he is fond of society, and could not exist on a remote farm several leagues from a neighbour, passing the greater part of his time within his own domestic circle. Like the French the Spaniards are social beings, and love towns and villages and groups of habitations. The plantations in Florida were with few exceptions cultivated by English settlers, or by those Spanish subjects who by an intercourse with Georgia, had adopted the American customs.

In anticipation of the exchange of flags, during the last two years of the Spanish government, those who had money or influence procured their surveys, such as they are ; but all could not be accommodated, nor was it material to the validity of their concessions by the laws and usages then existing. The returns of these surveys were by an authorised surveyor, who deposited his plat in the notarial office, being sworn previous to each location to the due performance of his duty.

With respect to the powers of the governors to make grants, it seems doubtful whether they had any other limit than the discretion of the confirming tribunals : although the author has taken much trouble, he has not been able to find whether they were limited to any extent in granting. Stoddard in his interesting sketches of Louisiana expresses an opinion, that the powers of the lieutenant-governors or sub-delegates were discretionary ; but from other sources we know, that about 1801 the governor of Louisiana was restricted in the extent of his grants, particularly to new settlers. From the best sources of information we find, that the governors of Florida were authorised from time to time to grant lands, by virtue of certain royal orders direct from the court of Madrid, to new settlers who became Spanish subjects, and the quantity granted was in proportion to the family and slaves held by the applicant. Grants to a large amount have been thus made by the governors, conditioned for the confirmation in proportion to the number of settlers or slaves brought in ; upon due proof of which, the number of acres *pro rata* were patented to the colonist with a royal title.

Any inhabitant or new comer could also obtain a grant for lands, on condition of his occupying, planting and cultivating the same for ten years, erecting buildings, &c. ; at the expiration of the time, upon sufficient proof, the royal title of full concession was made out to him : but many of the inhabitants who held lands under similar conditions, which had long been complied with, neglected to take out their royal or confirmatory titles, which under the Spanish government was not obligatory upon them, and besides the fees were somewhat expensive ; but upon the knowledge of the cession, numbers crowded to prove the fulfilment of their grants ; and most of the records from 1818 to 1821 are filled with royal titles predicated upon former conditional grants, the articles of which had been complied with.

The titles made by Spain, being held by the treaty binding on the United States, to the same extent that they would have been valid under the dominion of the former, will smooth all difficulties arising under patents dated previous to the 24th of January, 1818 ; but the many claims posterior to that period, which will be clamorously urged, will cause the treaty of cession to be brought up at a future day for construction, before the supreme court of the United States ; yet the question will never be fully set at rest, until Congress have invested the judicial departments of the government with authority to try and investigate it.

The boards of commissioners with their limited powers, are good enough for the purposes for which they were created ; to ascertain the quantity claimed under Spain, and to confirm their plain concessions ; but they have not power, nor can Congress give power to Commissioners *as such*, to adjudicate conclusively against the individuals.

Let us hope that the long contests in Louisiana and Missouri respecting land claims, may not be repeated in the case of Florida ; and that prompt and efficient measures may be laid, for the conclusive adjustment of all the titles in the territory : until this is done all population, all settlement will be withheld ; nor would the introduction of the public lands to the market tend to smooth difficulties : on the contrary it would only transfer the law suits to the purchasers. Disputes between the United States and a portion of the citizens of Missouri have existed nearly twenty years, originating in grants made by France and Spain.

The general proposition that a citizen should have a remedy to determine his rights, where the same subject happens to be claimed by both the government and the individual, appears too obviously just and necessary to require illustration in any ordinary case. In the determination of these claims Florida is materially interested : they are interspersed through a large portion of the territory, in all directions. The disputes that may and will arise on some or all of these claims, unless immediately adjusted, will have a tendency to prevent emigration, at least to the central parts, and to throw the population into distant detached settlements ; and will prevent some of the best land of the province from being brought into the market, peopled and cultivated.

The first years of the Spanish government after re-occupying the Floridas, seem to have passed away without many grants being made ; except confirming in their possessions, such of the British subjects who chose to remain upon their lands or lots. In the year 1793 a royal order came out from the Spanish court, authorising the governors to make grants to new settlers or inhabitants, conditioned for the performance of some acts of public utility or for the complete settlement of the lands.

Another ten years rolled away, and about 1803 a new order arrived, under which considerable tracts of land were granted : in 1809 a royal cedula appears to have authorised the issuing of grants as rewards for civil or military services ; and in 1815 another mandate from the king of Spain, authorised the governors to make concessions for similar services ; this latter order being issued upon the special representations made to the Spanish government, of the losses sustained by the inhabitants from the revolutionary proceedings of 1812. It is not distinctly understood to what amount the governors were limited ; probably the *quantum* was left to be decided upon by themselves, in proportion to the merits of the several applicants : in the list of grants issued as a reward for civil and military services, the largest quantity does not exceed fifty thousand acres, except in one instance, viz. the grant made on the 19th of November, 1810 by governor White, to Don Pedro Miranda, as a reward for his various services expressed in the concession.

The several orders to the governors or sub-delegates of Florida coming direct from Madrid, and regulating the mode of making grants in certain cases, do not appear to have interfered with the general standing instructions to these officers, for issuing concessions in the ordinary routine ; nor with the power of the governor-general and intendant of the island of Cuba, to order concessions to such persons as he judged proper : in virtue of this authority, the governor-general granted to the commercial house of Don Fernando de la Maza Arredondo and Son of the Havana, on the 17th of December, 1817, a large tract of country situated around the old Indian town of Alachua, upon the fulfilment of certain conditions. This immense concession has been surveyed, and Messrs. Arredondo and Son having sold out to various persons, settlements have been established upon it, and measures taken for the compliance with the terms of the grant, the period for which is extended by the terms of the treaty. Several companies have been formed for the

19

purpose of colonizing here ; one among the farmers of New-Jersey. another in New-York known as the *Florida Association*, &c.   The settlers upon this tract will form a centre for a population in the very heart of the country, should the measures of the government not be prejudicial to their intentions.

A recapitulation of the places upon which concessions have been made, will put into one view their extent.

The neck of land between the rivers St. Mary and St. John on the north and south, the Atlantic ocean on the east, and the King's road from the Cowford ferry to Coleraine on the west, is entirely covered by grants in occupancy and cultivation : this is the northern division mentioned in the historical observations.

South of this division the grants extend on both sides of the river St. John, as far almost as the head lake : upon Dunn's lake and Haw creek, and upon most of the other tributaries of St. John, particularly Pablo and Black creeks : over the plains of San Diego, and upon each branch of the North river : almost entirely through the Twelve-mile swamp and its ramifications : the principal part of all, and the entire of the choice lands southwardly, from St. Augustine to Tomoca river, east of the main road, besides the banks of all the small water courses.

The concessions are close together upon the front of Halifax river to Mosquito bar, and the deserted town of New Smyrna ; thence in a similar way to Mosquito south lagoon *and* the Haul-over isthmus ; and also occupy the rich hammocks or swamps running parallel to the coast, a mile or two west of the front water courses.   The banks of Indian river and its north-west branch, northwardly from the Haul-over are likewise occupied ; likewise southwardly, though not without some vacant spots to St. Sebastian river.

Thus far the concessions have been made without the old Indian boundary line ; whereby the peninsula from the head of St. John's river, and between the right bank of that stream and the Atlantic ocean, may be considered as almost entirely covered by various grants ; and it is a matter of question whether the federal government should or should not be at the expense of sectioning this and the preceding northern divisions of the territory : the surplus lands would invariably be of inferior quality and could never repay the expenses of the survey. On the other hand, if an act of Congress relative to this matter be carried into effect, it will be the means of settling the boundaries of numerous concessions which otherwise may long remain in suspense. This act provides that the public surveyors are to mark off each claim as allowed by the commissioners or otherwise :from the loose mode of surveying generally hitherto used in Florida, but a very small number of the few lines actually marked through the woods are distinct, and therefore almost all the located as well as the unlocated grants will require to be marked out ; which if done otherwise than by the government surveyors, at the contract price of four dollars per lineal mile, will put the proprietors to an enormous expense, which they are at present unable to afford : moreover if they are left to regulate their own surveys, litigations will unavoidably arise, which would be avoided were the location made by impartial persons, as the government surveyors cannot but be.

The application of the universal system of sectioning, would further produce an intimate topographical knowledge of the country, so highly desirable, that should the United States not carry it into effect, the author considers it a subject proper for the consideration of the territorial legislature : the local contribution, raised among the proprietors and claimants of the land within the district treated of, would be infinitely less to each individual, than the amount they would have to pay to their private surveyors ; and the country would at once be accurately known, the boundaries of each tract conclusively fixed, and general satisfaction would be produced.

Upon the western side of St. John's river the grants are much

less numerous, but are disposed over a large portion of country;
many are placed upon the shores of the Ocklawaha river, and not a
few through an imaginary hammock which was supposed to extend
from that stream to the Alachua territory : no such hammock is
known to exist ; but the creek which flows from the eastern end of
Orange lake into Ocklawaha river, called Orange lake creek, has a
narrow skirt of thick swamp on each side which the claimants of
the lands may probably not find so desirable as the rich luxuriant
hammock which they had been taught to expect.

Several large concessions are in the heart of the peninsula ;
among which particularly is the one upon Alligator creek of eight
miles square ; and the great Alachua grant before mentioned made
to Arredondo and Sons ; the Miranda grant, upon the waters of
Tampa and Hillsborough bays ; a grant upon the Coolasahatchie,
and some others.

During the period of the invasion of the Indian territory from
Georgia, a great number of tracts of land were run out in the Alachua
district for the conquerors, by surveyors whom they brought in their
train, of which plats were made ; the persons employed on these
surveys seem to have taken some pains to define the respective al-
lotments, for in traversing through the district, the lines are occasionally seen very distinct ; so that should the claimants come forward they will have much less difficulty in finding their lands than
many who have obtained grants under more peaceable circumstances. The author has been informed that copies of most of the
plats are in the hands of a gentleman in Georgia.

We shall conclude the account of the various grants of land made
in the Floridas, by giving the boundaries of the three celebrated
grants made to the Duke of Alagon, the Count of Punon Rostro, and
to Don Pedro de Vargas, respectively. The two latter individuals
received compensation for what they were deprived of by the
treaty, but the Duke of Alagon having fallen into disgrace, received

not the equivalent he was entitled to by the new constitution of Spain, and it is said that his remonstrance upon the stretch of power used by Ferdinand the seventh in depriving him of his lands, caused his banishment. Whatever was the cause of his losing the smiles of his royal master, it is well known that he is now in exile in one of the Italian states, and under the *surveillance* of the Spanish minister. How precarious is the tenure by which a courtier holds his unenviable situation!

GRANT TO THE DUKE OF ALAGON.

This grant appears to have been made upon the 17th of December, 1817, in consequence of the Duke's application made on the 12th of July preceding : Letters patent were issued on the 6th of February, 1818, to the governor of Cuba and the council of Indies to give effect to the grant and on the 26th of June of the same year formal possession of the lands was delivered to the Duke's agent by the governor of East Florida. These lands according to the words of the concession include—" All the uncultivated land not ceded in East Florida, which lies between the rivers Saint Lucie and St. John, as far as the mouths by which they empty themselves into the sea and the coast of the gulf of Florida, and the adjacent islands, with the mouth of the river Hijuelos in the 26th degree of latitude, following the left bank up to its source ; drawing a line from lake Macaco, then descending by the way of the river St. John to the lake Valdez, crossing by another line from the extreme north of the said lake to the source of the river Amanina, following its right bank as far as its mouth in the 28th deg. 25th min. of north latitude, and running along the sea coast, with all the adjacent islands up to the mouth of the river Hijuelos."

Of this large concession the Duke of Alagon after the confirmation of the treaty by the United States in 1819, but before the explanatory ratification by the king which annulled his grant, conveyed the western portion to Richard S. Hackley an American citizen and formerly consul from the United States at Cadiz : the extent of the lands held by Mr. Hackley is marked upon the map of Florida.

GRANT TO THE COUNT OF PUNON ROSTRO.

This grant was also made on the 7th December, 1817, upon the same day with the concession to the duke of Alagon, in consequence of a petition presented by the count upon the 3d day of November preceding : this grant does not appear to have been perfected : it includes—" All the vacant lands not heretofore ceded in Florida, lying between the river Perdido, westward of the gulf of Mexico and the rivers Amanina and St. John, from Poppa* to the point where it empties into the ocean for the eastern limits ; and for the northern, the boundary line of the United States ; and to the south by the gulf of Mexico, including the desert islands on the coast."

It has been said that the count of Punon Rostro was indemnified for the loss of this concession, by a large grant of crown lands in the heart of old Spain ; which to him was doubtless no disagreeable exchange : besides he appears never to have taken possession of the lands, or done any other act of ownership.

GRANT TO DON PEDRO DE VARGAS.

The petition for this grant was not made until the 25th January, 1818, and the concession issued on the 2d of February : the gift bestowed upon this favored courtier is described as being " The property of the land which lies comprised within the followtng limits, that is to say : from the mouth of the river Perdido and its bay in the gulf of Mexico following the sea coast, to ascend by the bay of Buen

---

* *Poppa* is the name of an antient Spanish fortification on the west bank of St. John's river opposite to *Picolati,* where there was a ferry : these two forts are situated at the north end-of a large bay of the river, which extends south as far as the old fort of *Buena Vista :* this bay was formerly called *Lake Valdez.*

Socorro and of Mobile, continuing by the river Mobile until it touches the northern line of the United States, and descending by that in a right line to the source of the river Perdido, and following the said river Perdido in its lower part, and the bay of that name returns by the sea coast towards the west, comprehending all the creeks, entries and the islands adjacent, which may belong to Spain at the present time till it reaches the west line of the United States, then returning by th ir northern line, comprehending all the vacant lands which belong or may belong to Spain, and are in dispute or reclamation with the United States according to the tenor of the treaties : and also all the vacant lands not ceded to any other individual which are between the river Hijuelos in East Florida and the river St. Lucie, drawing a line from the source of one river to the source of the other, and following by the coast of the gulf of Mexico from the mouth of the Hijuelos to the point of Tancha, and doubling this by the coast of the gulf of Florida to the mouth of the river St. Lucie with the islands and keys adjacent.'' The equivalent given to Don Pedro de Vargas for the annulment of this grant was according to report an extensive monopoly in certain branches of commerce in the Spanish colonies ; which upon reflecting that the principal part of this immense concession (comprehending all the counties of Escambia, Jackson and Duval, and large parts of St. John's county together with the lands in dispute now part of Alabama) is after all dubious both as to right of granting and good quality, and point of time, was a most superabundant remuneration.

In the early grants the amount of land conceded appears to have been computed in *cavallerias* and sometimes in *peonias*. The estimation of the former in Florida is that it contains thirty-three and one-third American acres : of the latter the relative value is one-fourth of the former.

By the law of the Indies (*Recopilacion de las leyes de los Indios* published at Madrid in 1776, a work similar to a digest of the statutes of one of our states, a *peonia* is described to be " a lot of fifty feet wide and one hundred deep : cultivatable ground for one hundred bushels (*fanegas*) of wheat (*trigo*) or barley (*cebada*) ; for ten of Indian corn : two roods (*huebras*) of land for a kitchen garden (*huerta*) ; and eight for saplings of fruit trees (*arboles de secadal*) : pasture land for ten breeding sows (*puercas de vientre*) : twenty cows and five mares (*yeguas* ; one hundred sheep and twenty goats." By the same statute a *cavalleria* is defined as containing a lot of one hundred feet wide and two hundred deep, and in all other respects equal to five *Peonias*.

In the island of Cuba the lands are granted in a circular form : the location being determined by fixing upon a known spot as a centre, and the terms of the concession are so much lineal distance upon each point of the compass (*sobre cada viento.*) These circles are supposed to be tangential, and the spaces between them are called *tierras realengas*, (vacant or royal lands.) But as they actually intersect each other in almost every instance, endless lawsuits, disputes and contentions arise. Probably to obviate this, or perhaps to comply with the usual mode of laying out lands in Florida, the very few grants which have been made in this mode specify that they are to be equal to a grant of so far *sobre cada viento*, but to be laid out in a square form.*

————

In concluding these observations upon the Floridas, and their various resources, which have been drawn up from a variety of documents published and unpublished, as well as from the numerous

* The author in the first part of these observations upon land titles, derived much assistance from the interesting speech made by Mr. Barton in the house of representatives in congress, when treating of the Louisiana land claims ; the circumstances were so very applicable to Florida that many of the remarks have been closely copied. This ought to have been acknowledged in the Introduction.

notes taken by the author and his friends in the territory, he respectfully entreats that the public will discriminate between what he has stated as actually *now* to be found in Florida, and the inferences he has drawn as to what it is capable of being made.

So many false lights are held out upon the opening of a new country to induce emigration thither, that he feels a natural anxiety lest what he has pointed out as the probable future, may be interpreted as the existing present. In dividing his remarks he has endeavoured to obviate this impression, and he momentarily intrudes to remove it.

Florida is now a republic; unshackled by the restrictions of a monarch, or the despotic sway of an inquisitorial governor, who in many instances united the legislative, judicial and executive powers, it will soon develope the real extent of its capabilities.

The sanguine disposition of some may carry them in their enterprises beyond the bounds of prudence, and their failure in certain cases may be quoted against the country : caution and prejudice may withhold numbers from joining the population or embarking in any but certain undertakings ; but enough will be found whose enterprise, energy, and perseverance, will place things in their proper light and prove the general truth of the propositions which have been advanced in favour of the Floridas.

With a superficial extent larger than the state of New-York, with a climate in most parts as salubrious as the rest of the United States, with a soil capable of producing more than one lucrative staple, it is surely no visionary hope that we indulge when we look forward beyond the few years that are to intervene before FLORIDA takes her natural post of importance in the FEDERAL UNION.

END OF THE OBSERVATIONS

ERRATTA.

Page 8, line 22,	for *recourses,*	read resources.
,, 17, ,, 7,	,, *1638,*	,, 1538.
,, 19, ,, 14,	,, *previous,*	,, previous to.
,, 20, ,, 10,	,, *carry,*	,, convey.
,, 22, ,, 1,	,, *Maine,*	,, main.
,, 30, ,, 13,	,, *conflexion,*	,, confliction.
,, 30, ,, 15,	,, *successfully,*	,, successively.
,, 32, ,, 12,	,, *a,*	,, the.
,, 41, ,, 9,	,, *northerly,*	,, northwardly.
,, 42, ,, 5,	,, *spreads,*	,, spread.
,, 45, ,, 10,	,, *there,*	,, thence.
,, 45, ,, 31,	,, *pine,*	,, fine.
,, 50, ,, 2,	,, *there but,*	,, there the hammocks are [but.
,, 50, ,, 4,	,, *closing,*	,, clothing.
,, 55, ,, 8,	,, *lines,*	,, line.
,, 58, ,, 15,	,, *disunion,*	,, diversion.
,, 59, ,, 11,	,, *Appalachicola,*	,, Choctaw.
,, 61, and other places,	*Chamiooly,*	,, Chipola.
,, 62, line 16,	for *ages,*	,, time.

,, 64, at the top, { *should read as follows :* different sizes which Brandy creek falling into the St. Mary's seems to separate : the western subdivision between, &c.

,, 66, line 29,	for *gives,*	read give.
,, 69, ,, 21,	,, *an,*	,, one.
,, 75, ,, 5,	,, *a*	,, the.
,, 75, ,, 19,	,, *circuitous,*	,, crooked.
,, 77, ,, 17,	,, *renders,*	,, render.
,, 78, ,, 20,	,, *lamina,*	,, laminæ.
,, 80, ,, 24,	,, *or,*	,, through.
,, 81, ,, 16,	,, *principlo,*	,, principal.
,, 81, ,, 20,	,, *the small,*	,, similar.
,, ~~87,~~ ,, 4,	~~The auxiliary verbs should be in the plural number.~~	
,, 89, ,, 19,	for 68,	read 77.
,, 92, ,, 16,	,, *tract,*	,, coat.
,, 95, ,, 6,	,, *lead,*	,, led.
,, 100, ,, 20,	,, *little,*	,, tithe.
,, 105, ,, 14,	,, *remarkable,*	,, profitable.
,, 105, ,, 25,	,, *fine,*	,, five.
,, 106, ,, 27,	,, *this,*	,, the.
,, 110, ,, 29,	,, *has,*	,, had.
,, 112, ,, 30,	,, *must,*	,, may.
,, 120, ,, 17,	,, *fine,*	,, five.
,, 124, ,, 1,	,, *other,*	,, various.
,, 124, ,, 5,	,, *from,*	,, form.
,, 125, ,, 2,	,, *haunts,*	,, keys.
,, 127, ,, 12,	,, *all,*	,, any one.
,, 137, ,, 5,	,, *reflection,*	,, reflectors.
,, 146, ,, 24,	,, *lagoon to,*	,, lagoon and.
,, 147, ,, 11,	,, *otherwise, from,*	,, otherwise : from.
,, 151, ,, 21,	,, *Dural,*	,, Duval.
,, 151, ,, 23	,, *lads,*	,, lands.
,, 152, in the note	,, *Barbour,*	,, Barton.

FLORIDA.

———

SHORTLY after returning to England in 1823, Charles Blacker Vignoles prepared several articles for the *Encyclopaedia Metropolitana* (29 vols., London, 1817–1845). He wrote most of them himself: "Cumberland," "Curaçao," "St. Croix," "Creole," "Crane," "Docks," "Dominica," "Georgia," and "Guadeloupe"; but he co-authored articles on Florida and Cuba with a Dr. Bonnycastle. The article on Florida is virtually a condensation of Vignoles' *Observations upon the Floridas*, and it is therefore one of the first articles to appear in an encyclopedia on the subject of Florida as a possession of the United States.

FLORIDA.

———

FLORIDA at present principally consists of the long peninsula which proceeding from the South-Eastern part of the North American Continent, on the parallel of the 31st degree of North latitude, extends toward the West India Islands, to within half a degree of the Tropic of Cancer; being upwards of 400 miles in length from North to South, and having an average breadth of about 100 miles. This peninsular portion is now the limit of *East Florida*. The Atlantic Ocean bounds the peninsula on the East, on the South the Gulf Stream divides it from the Island of Cuba, and the waters of the Gulf of Mexico wash the Western shores; the boundaries to the North is the State of Georgia; and from the North-Western angle the remaining portion of the Country, known as *West Florida*, stretches Westward, bounded on the North first by Georgia, and next by the State of Alabama, which also flanks it to the West, the bay and river of Perdido being the boundary. West Florida extends nearly 300 miles from East to West, being however not more than 40 or 50 miles wide from the shores of the Gulf of Mexico on the South, to the boundary lines on the North. The river Appalachicola formerly constituted the Western limit of East Florida, but since the cession of the country by Spain to the United States of America, the division has been moved Eastward to the river Suwanee or Little San Juan. Florida once extended as far West as the Mississippi River, but since the peace of 1783 the bay and river Perdido have been determined as its Western limit. The Floridas, by the most recent published map, (1823,) appear to contain an area of about 50,000 square miles.

Florida was first seen in 1497 by Cabot; but it does not appear that the country was either named or explored, until Don Juan Ponce de Leon landed in April, 1512. His arrival took place, according to Herrera, on Saturday the 2nd of April, 1512, in 30° 8' North latitude, having previously on the Sunday before (Palm Sunday) discovered an island off the coast from which he had been driven by bad weather. Palm Sunday in Spanish is called *Pasqua de Resurecion*, or commonly *Flores*; whence, observes the Historian, De Leon, seeing that the country he had discovered was very beautiful, with flowering groves, and fair (Florida) to look on, as well as in devout remembrance of the holy season at which he had achieved his wishes, he called it Florida.* Ponce de Leon was so well satisfied with his discovery, that he repaired to Spain, and obtained permission to conquer and govern it, and in 1513 returned with three vessels; but instead of reaping the rich reward for his toils which he expected, he encountered a courageous race of Indians, who repulsed all his attempts, and, having slain the greatest part of his army, forced him to hasten his return to Cuba. Seven years afterwards, the pilot, Mirvelo, visited the country, and having been favourably received, reported such wonders, that several of the rich merchants of San Domingo equipped two ships to traffic with the natives. Some of these unhappy natives were cajoled on board these vessels, which immediately sailed with them, and a few pearls, skins, and some silver, which the adventurers had obtained. Only one of these corsair ships arrived in Hispaniola, and the unfortunate Indians it car-

---

* *La llamaron la Florida, porque tenia muy linda vista de muchas y frescas arboledas, y era llana y pareja; y porque tambien la descubrieron en tiempo de Pasqua Florida, se quiso Juan Ponce conformar en el nombre, con estas dos razones.* The learned French Translator of the *Florida del Ynca* has thrown away much trouble and calculation, in endeavouring to prove that the Inca was wrong in stating that this country was discovered on the 27th of March, 1513, on which day, he observes, Palm Sunday did not occur. The Inca mistook the second voyage of De Leon for his first discovery.

ried afterwards died of despair. After this visit, Vasquez Lucas De Ayllon in 1524 solicited permission to establish the Spanish power in Florida. His request was granted by the Emperor, and Ayllon, with Mirvelo, set forth from San Domingo. He was repulsed, as De Leon had been, by the valiant Aborigines; but this new misfortune did not hinder Panfilo de Narvaez from invading their country in 1528. He perished during his navigation of the coast.

Fernando de Soto in 1539, with a very considerable force, and assisted by Moscoso, attempted the conquest of Florida. After a long and very able trial, he, as well as his forerunners, was totally foiled. The History of his wars is written by a Portuguese gentleman of Elvas, who accompanied him, and had Soto succeeded, he would have deserved equal notice with Cortez and Pizarro.

On the failure of Soto, many chieftains applied to Charles V. for leave to conquer these Indians; but the Emperor would not permit any new attempts, and in 1549 he sent Cancel Balbastro, a Dominican friar, as superior, with missionaries, who undertook their conversion. Balbastro was killed with two of his fraternity, and the rest flying to their ships, hastily left the coast, and returned to Spain; telling the Emperor as their excuse, according to Garcillasso, that they had left the Barbarians because they found their hearts hardened, and that they took no pleasure in hearing the word. Mehendez and several others tried their fortunes in Florida afterwards, but the Spanish power never gained a very firm footing in the country until in comparatively recent times.

From the year 1543, when the remnant of Soto's force under Moscoso reached Mexico in their flight from Florida, the French, the English, and the Spaniards, were continually at variance about that country. In 1564 it was partly occupied by some French adventurers, who were attacked by Spanish troops from the West Indies, and defeated. Such prisoners as were taken were hung with labels about their necks, bearing the inscription, *Not as Frenchmen but as Heretics.* Dominic de Gourges, a native of Gascony, fired with indignation at this outrage, disposed of his property, built some vessels, and choosing a band of determined spirits like himself, sailed to avenge his slaughtered countrymen. He overthrew the Spaniards at all points, and after displaying great valour he also hung all his prisoners, with this sentence attached to their necks, *Not as Spaniards but as Assassins,* destroyed all the fortified places, and, being unprotected by France, left the country. Thus the settlement of the Spaniards in Florida did not finally succeed until 1665, when they fortified the Capital, St. Augustine. This place suffered repeated attacks from the Buccaneers and neighbouring Colonists, and was besieged ineffectually by the Governor of Carolina for three months in 1702.

In 1740 it underwent another siege from the English troops under General Oglethorpe; but the Floridas remained Spanish colonies till 1763, when they were ceded to Great Britain in exchange for the Havanna. They were, however, recovered by Spain in 1781, and confirmed to her by the Peace of 1783. In 1810 a revolution broke out in West Florida, and the leaders sent a request to the United States to be admitted to the Union. Measures were taken to occupy the country, in pursuance of a claim which the Government of the United States asserted it had on that portion of Florida since the year 1801, when it purchased Louisiana from France. Whilst these events were occurring, a Treaty was set on foot with Spain, for the cession of East Florida; and the American Cabinet, unable longer to throw a veil over its desires, despatched General Jackson with a force to take possession of Pensacola, which he did in 1818. This act was afterwards disavowed by the President, though with how little truth has since been discovered; as the territory of Florida has been annexed to the Union, through the weakness of impoverished and impotent Spain, and the difficulties in which so many years of war had plunged the rest of Europe.

The prevalent feature of the Floridas is flatness: sand and lands covered with the pine growth, present to the eye of a stranger at its first aspect an appearance of sterility, which on examination is found to have conveyed a false impression. A remarkable characteristic of the country is the majestic and imposing appearance of many of the rivers for a short distance from their mouths, which give the promise of a vast length from sources originating in interior mountains. After pursuing their course upwards for a short distance the stream contracts, and soon dwindles into a narrow creek, issuing from some interminable marsh. The rivers St. John and St. Lucia are striking instances of this kind; as are all the rivers on the Southern coast. Florida possesses also a peculiarity of formation, on the Atlantic shores, common to Georgia and the Carolinas, namely, a natural chain of water communication parallel to the sea-coast. From the North of the river St. Mary's an inland navigation exists, between the sea islands and the ocean, to St. John's River. A creek entering this river, flows parallel to the shore towards the head of another creek which falls into the harbour of St. Augustine, and a very short cut made here would complete the inland navigation from this town to Charleston. A similar passage between the islands and the main land proceeds to the Southward as far as Matanza. A short cut is here requisite to complete the communication to To-moka. From the latter spot the navigation is uninterrupted, (with the exception of a small portage behind Cape Canaveral, of 660 yards,) for 200 miles. These channels receive the name of river, narrow, sound, or lagoon, according to their appearance. At Ju-piter Inlet, in latitude 27° North, the chain is once more inter-rupted, and would require a short artificial opening. Hence a series of lakes and creeks continue the natural line of boat navi-gation, with little or no interruption, to the inlet of New River, within a very short distance of the Cape Florida settlements. During the period in which piratical cruisers remained on the coast of Florida, General Coppinger, the Governor resident at Augustine, communicated with the Havanna by means of this series of water courses. A light boat, manned with six stout and trusty men, and commanded by an experienced pilot, to whom the despatches were intrusted, went down the narrows from St. Au-gustine to Matanza Inlet, and passing out to sea, kept within a few boats' length of the shore, until opposite the head of the next inland navigation. The boat was then beached, and hauled for a quarter of a mile over the portage, and again launched. This was repeated at the harbour near Cape Canaveral. On arriving at Jupiter Inlet, (the mouth of which is generally closed,) the canoe was hauled over the beach, and put to sea. Hence the messengers crept along the shore until they were opposite the nearest prac-ticable navigation, and thus proceeded to Cape Florida; here they procured a larger boat, and navigating among the keys, kept out of the influence of the Gulf Stream, until opposite the Havanna, which they reached in a few hours' sail, at night. In this manner the writer of this Paper explored the rivers and coast in 1821, 1822. There is a somewhat similar formation existing on the coast of West Florida, from Appalachia to Pensacola Bays, but it is by no means so connected. The Eastern coast of the internal Prov-inces North of Mexico from Galveston Bay to Tampico, have a similar series of natural waterways running parallel to the sea-coast. It is further remarkable, that the long strips of land next the sea are low, flat, and sandy, while the edge of the main land is almost invariably formed into a low bluff, about eight or ten feet above the surface of the water, and sometimes rising into high sand-cliffs.

The country to the Westward of the river St. John is the most interesting part of Florida. It is intersected by an irregular ridge, or rather an extent of undulating ground, which separates the waters discharging into the East and West sides of the peninsula. Spurs or branches run up between the several streams that run parallel to each other, and on both sides of isolated rivers. To the Southward this *plateau* of broken ground expands very considerably, and was formerly covered with Indian villages, some of which still exist; but the ridges gradually sink, until they are lost in the vast Savannas behind Tampa Bay. Most of this part of the country is beautiful and fertile, containing large bodies of oak and hickory lands, with pine-bearing lands of a rich soil, based on lime-stone. Over the whole surface, and also in some parts of West Florida which resemble this district, Nature has scattered a number of wells, holes, and ponds, of all sizes and various depths, many of them sufficiently deep, when protected with the shade of the surrounding growth, to resist the exhausting evaporations of the summer sun, becoming reservoirs of water which is cool in the warmest day. Some of them have their banks of such a slope as to allow cattle to descend to the water; others are of so perpendicular and so narrow an aperture, as to form complete natural wells, which require the use of a rope and bucket; and all are distinguished by a tuft of hummock trees, growing around even the smallest, giving a pleasing variety to the monotony of the pine woods. Besides the smaller ponds, a larger kind are often met with, romantic in their appearance, and approaching to the dignity of lakes. In some of these are islands, abounding with groves of the wild orange trees.

The great Savannas of Florida form one more predominant feature on the face of the country. After periods of heavy falls of rain, they become deeply inundated; when the warm seasons have evaporated this deluge, they are so desiccated, that whenever fire is put to the exterior it sweeps down the tall grass instantaneously, and a fresh covering of tender herbage or odoriferous flowers succeeds. It was soon after one of these *burns* that the elder Bartram, in 1764, 1765, saw the great Alachua Savanna, of which he has given so glowing a description. Bartram, as a Botanist and an enthusiast, has written his celebrated *Travels* in so florid a style as to have created a suspicion of his veracity.

The writer of this Paper, however, has invariably found his facts, when abstracted from the flowery embroidery of his language, to be correct, and in the town in which the veteran traveller still lives, his name and Truth appear to be identified.

The soil of the Floridas is almost universally light; sands of various granulations, and sandy loam based upon lime-stone at very different depths; and from this lightness the lands are probably, with some exceptions, not capable of bearing a succession of exhausting crops; but when thrown into fallow, or, according to the phrase of the Southern States, into *old fields*, a fertilizing principle generated by the saline particles brought from the sea on both sides of the peninsula, which pervades the air, and subsides to the earth, quickly renovates the soil.

The different qualities of Florida lands may be classed distinctly under the following heads:

High Grounds.	Low Grounds.
Flat Pine Lands.	Pine Land Savannas.
Undulating Pine Lands.	Hummock Savannas.
Low Hummock.	River Swamps.
High Hummock.	Cypress Swamps.
Oak and Hickory Lands.	Fresh Marshes.
Scrub Lands.	Salt Marshes.

The *Flat Pine Lands* are of two kinds: one sort covered with a thick undergrowth of berry and palmetto bushes and dwarf laurel, the pine trees being only sparely scattered on the ground; the other sort has no undergrowth, but abounds in savannas and cypress ponds,—the herbage is luxuriant.

The *Undulating Pine Lands* are healthy and beautiful, the timber is tall, straight, and of a fine quality; succulent grass grows luxuriantly, no undergrowth is seen, except around the pools before described.

The *Low Hummock* is the richest soil, and capable of producing for many successive years abundant crops of sugar, corn, hemp, or other equally exhausting productions. The growth upon them is principally the cabbage tree or palmetto, (of which it may be observed that none are found except in the peninsula part of Florida,) ash, mulberry, dogwood, Spanish oak, lime oak, white oak, swamp hickory, sweet bay, sassafras, cedar, magnolia (*Grandiflora*) fig, orange, prickly ash, and a vast number of other kinds with numerous varieties of each: in the more Southern latitudes the torch tree, gum guiacum, mastic, tamarind, red-stopper, pigeon plum, cocoa plum, sea grapes, ziswood, &c. A thick vegetable mould from one to two feet in depth covers the surface; below, black sand, gradually becoming paler as the depth increases.

The *High Hummocks* are even more dense in the growth than the others, but the coat of vegetable matter is thin, and the white sand lies within 12 or 18 inches of the surface; notwithstanding, the lands continue productive for a length of time. In addition to most of the trees found in the low hummocks, we may add laurel, red oak, chestnut oak, Chinquapine or dwarf chestnut, beech, persimmon, cinnamon, laurel, bastard ash, myrrh, locust, and a numerous list of other trees: countless parasitical plants interweave and fold round the trees: the vine shoots up to a most surprising height, and the stalk is commonly found seven and eight inches in diameter.

The *Oak and Hickory Lands* produce almost exclusively those two forest trees, occasionally mingled with gigantic pines; the undergrowth consists of sucker saplings of oak and hickory. The black oak is most abundant: the soil is a rich, deep, yellow, sandy loam.

The *Scrub Lands* are generally undulating; a small and ferruginous sand covers their surface, an infinite variety of dwarf oak shrubs and creeping plants form their covering; occasionally clusters of the spruce pine grow on the highest ridges, which die after attaining the height of 20 or 30 feet. Water is scarce, and the whole appearance is forbidding, presenting no probability of advantage to the settler, except that of raising hogs, which would thrive on the acorns of the dwarf oaks, and the roots of the sandy plants.

The *Pine Land Savannas* are merely ponds or drains in winter, covered in the dry season with rich crops of natural grass.

The *Hummock Savannas* are more fertile; fossil broken shells are embedded in the rich black mould, based on clay. Pasturage of the most luxuriant kind is afforded by these grounds.

The word *swamp* is in the signification now adopted in America peculiar to the country; a *swamp* is understood to be a tract of land lying low, but with a sound bottom, covered, however, in rainy seasons with water.

River Swamps are annually overflowed, and when brought into cultivation require embankments. The growth common in these swamps are oaks, maple, tupelo, elder, willow, swamp magnolia, black birch, sumac, cypress, black and white poplar, Florida holly, sycamore, hawthorn, &c. Sometimes the land immediately on the river banks is high, and the back swamp very low, and always inundated.

Cypress Swamps are mostly near the heads of rivers, and in a constant state of inundation; with no underbush, but crowds of the cypress shoots or *knees*, pointing up like small pyramids. The *Fresh Marshes* are distinguished into hard and soft, and, when drained and embanked, are fertile, particularly the latter.

The *Salt Marshes*, both hard and soft, are similar to those of Georgia and South Carolina; but in that part of the peninsula South of Mosquito, the mangrove takes the place of the marsh grass and reeds, increasing in size as it approaches the Tropic. In latitude 29° the mangrove is but a bush; on the banks of the Orinoco it becomes a gigantic tree. When the main stem of a mangrove gains a little height it sends down to the water a new shoot or rest, and each horizontal branch as it puts forth does the same, surrounding the parent trunk like the offspring of the Indian banyan tree; these downward shoots, as they approach the water, branch into several points, which again subdivide almost *ad infinitum;* these become closer interwoven with similar ramifications from the surrounding trees, and often totally obstruct the narrow channels or creeks whose waters, in times of freshets and floods, ooze through the roots as through a thousand miniature arches.

Four strata usually compose the soil of the Florida lands: an upper coating of vegetable mould or earth; below, sand; beyond, a layer of marl or clay; and lowest, indurations of shell and lime-stone rocks. This order is varied; some of the High Hummocks have deep beds of rich loamy, black sand, thickly overspread, and mingled with decomposed fossil and periwinkle shells, and below sand only. As a general remark, it is certain that the clay and lime-stone retain the moisture from oozing through the sands, which are therefore fertile when based on those harder substrata.

The various trees before mentioned appear to be natives; but it was doubted whether the orange was an indigene, for although found in every part, yet it is only where the Indians may have scattered the seeds; in those places which these wanderers have seldom frequented, though far South, the orange is rarely, if ever found; where man has not penetrated with the fruit in his hand, the tree is unknown. The two kinds of Florida orange most common are the sour and the bitter-sweet, or Seville orange. Gallnuts are produced in the dwarf oaks. Hops are said to be indigenous, but they are seldom met with; the starry aniseed, or *somo* or *skimmi* of Japan and China, has been found, and many plants of these two Countries are commonly met with in Florida.

Such is the natural growth of Florida, the products of artificial culture are very numerous. The cotton plant has been already extensively cultivated, and its produce is well known in the markets of Charleston and Savanna. Sugar is already successfully produced, and will become the great staple product of the Country. Tobacco, if renewed frequently by fresh seed from Cuba, equals the produce of that Island. The grape, the olive, the Levant currant (*Vilis apyrena*) will succeed; in short, the list of fruits, gums, and medicinal plants would fill pages. Indian corn, buck wheat, and Guinea corn, are the principal bread stuffs. Rye and oats have been introduced. The artificial grasses, particularly the Carolina dog-grass, will grow in every situation. It is highly probable the tea plant would succeed, but the attempt is yet unmade.

The climate of the whole of Florida during eight months of the year, from October to June, is delightful, and one continued Spring; the range of the thermometer in the hot summer months is only from 84° to 88° of Fahrenheit; and the intense sultry weather of Carolina and Georgia is seldom felt, except during a South or South-West wind, which impedes on the Atlantic side the action of the sea breeze, and acts as a sirocco.

The Spring and summer are usually dry; the autumns changeable; and the winters mild, and even serene. Snow is scarcely seen at St. Augustine twice in a century, but the black frost is an occasional visitor, though at the severest times the ice has never formed thicker than the sixteenth of an inch; beyond Cape Canaveral it is unknown, but the nipping of the white frost is felt in some years as far as the extreme capes of Florida. The duration of frost or cold lasts but a few hours, occurring usually in January. The coldest winds are from the North-West.

In the peninsula of Florida rain is foretold one or two days before it falls, either by an immoderate dew, or on a calm night by a total absence of the dews; the North-East winds are cool and moist, with frequent rain, but almost invariably when the passing shower has fallen, the heavens clear up, and the breezes which brought the moisture blow free and unsurcharged with clouds. The rains and dews, without being troublesome, create at most seasons such a luxuriant vegetation, that the surface of the earth is never without good verdure. The long absence of the sun in these latitudes gives the ground time to cool and to recover from the daily evaporations; hence also the delightful freshness of the nights in the most sultry periods of the year.

In the course of the first American war, the IXth regiment of British Infantry was stationed in various parts of East Florida, and during a period of 20 months it did not lose a man, except from accident. The night air is not hurtful at any season; the inhabitants and strangers constantly walking till late on summer and autumnal evenings with impunity.

The principal river of East Florida is the *St. John's*, which will be best described from its mouth upwards; this embouchure lies in latitude 30° 18' North, longitude 81° 34' West, with 12 feet water on its bar at ordinary tides, the breadth being one mile. For 30 miles the course is at right angles to the shore, with large expansive reaches filled with islands. At the Cowford Ferry the stream narrows to 1000 yards, and the direction becomes parallel to the line of the sea-coast, the current flowing due North; for the next 30 or 40 miles a succession of deep bays characterises the stream, being from three to six miles in breadth. In the old Maps these indentations are delineated and named as actual lakes. At the Alachua Ferry the river begins to contract and wind in reaches, but it soon expands again at the mouth of the Ockla-waha River. Lake George is a beautiful piece of water, 18 miles in length, and eight or nine wide, and terminates the chain of lakes; the river beyond is narrow, not exceeding the breadth of the Thames at Richmond. Above Hope Hill settlement, where the first sugar cane was planted in East Florida, the stream is from the South-East, rapidly contracting, and at length, on reaching a lake of about three miles in diameter, is totally lost in latitude 28° 40' North. This lake is situated in the midst of a marsh, on which the water is several feet in depth, flowing through the reeds and grass with considerable velocity. The extent of this marsh is scarcely defined, but there is but little doubt that it extends longitudinally and parallel to the coast as far as the great Southern morasses. The St. John's is navigable for sloops to Lake George, and for boats drawing five feet water to the head lake. The distance from which to the sea, including the sinuosities of the stream, is little less than 180 miles.

The *Suwanee*, or *Little St. John's River*, ranks next in importance. Three principal branches from this stream; the chief, or Eastern, extends through and forms the sole outlet for the great Oke-fin-o-cau Swamp. This swamp has formerly received various other names, but the orthography appears now to be settled.

(See EKANFANOGA.) The middle branch takes the name of *Alapaha*, and has numerous arms coming from the Southern part of Georgia. The Western arm is called the *Onithlacucly*. The conjoint waters flow nearly South, and discharge themselves into the Gulf of Mexico in latitude 29° 23' North, longitude 83° 22' West, after a course of 200 miles.

The river *Ocklockoune* is another large river flowing out of Georgia; it is already a stream of importance when entering Florida, and after running South-West 40 or 50 miles it turns to the South-East, and falls into Appalachia Bay, behind James's Island, in latitude 30° 9' North and longitude 84° 17' West.

The river *Appalachicola* is formed by the junction of two larger streams at Fort Nicholo, in latitude 30° 43' North, longitude 84° 54' West, where it enters Florida precisely at the South-West angle of Georgia. The course is thence nearly South; it receives the Ocapilca and Wemico from the Westward, rolls down a vast volume of water to its mouth behind Cape St. Blas in the Gulf of Mexico, in latitude 29° 50' North, longitude 84° 48' West.

Numerous other rivers water the plains of West Florida, of which the principal, the *Ekanfiuna*, discharges itself into the head of St. Andrew's Bay; the *Choctaw*, a powerful river, falls into Santa Rosa Bay; the *Yellow Water* and *Escambia Rivers* empty themselves into the Bay of Pensacola; and the *Perdido* into the bay of that name.

The *Santa Fè* or *Santaffy*, is a large branch of the Suwanee, coming from the Eastward, and almost uniting with the head branches of one of the tributary creeks of St. John's River.

The *Ocklawaha River* is the principal branch of the St. John's; its course is semicircular, having its source in about latitude 28° 20', in similar and connected marshes with that river. Length about 140 miles.

The *Amanina River* is a small but beautiful stream, emptying itself into the Gulf of Mexico, in about latitude 28½° North. The *Hillsborough* and *Manatee Rivers* empty themselves into Tampa Bay.

Charlotte River which falls into Charlotte Harbour and *Gallivan River*, discharging itself into Chatham Bay, on the Gulf of Mexico, both originate from a collection of waters known as Lake Macaco, or Spirito Santo, the exact situation of which is unknown. It is most probable that this lake is a low spot among the many marshes of the interior of the Southern point of the peninsula of Florida.

From the mouth of the Gallivan, behind Cape Romano, in latitude 26°, on the Western coast to the same parallel on the Atlantic Ocean, and still further Northward, all the streams originate in one vast swamp or inundated region, known as the Glades, *The Ever Glades;* the general appearance is a flat sandy surface, mixed with large stones and rocks covered with water to various depths; among which grows a remarkably strong water grass, shaped like a bayonet, and jagged at the edges, and so thickly set as to impede any passage even in a boat, unless where a current exists. This curious region is sprinkled with pine and hummock islands, and indented by promontories from the surrounding coast or shore. Towards its Northern extremity it becomes considerably contracted, and sends out several branches, one of which runs parallel to the Atlantic shore, and gives birth to many small rivers, and another gradually changing its character extends to the great swamps and Savannas which form the sources of the rivers St. John and Ocklawaha. The main body of this immense reservoir is supposed to cover an area of nearly 3000 square miles; and the branches contain, probably, nearly as large a surface in their aggregate extent.

Of the numerous rivers emanating from the Ever Glades, the following are the most remarkable: *Hijuelos,* or *Young River,* terminating in Chatham Bay; *Shark River,* emptying itself immediately to the North of Cape Sable, the South-West point of the peninsula; *Lemon River;* the *Rio Ratones,* at the back of Cape Florida, in latitude 25° 38' on the Atlantic shore; and all the other rivers on that coast as far as Jupiter Inlet. A singularity attends the mouths of these rivers, which is, that they are frequently closed. Their languid current is often unable to keep open the rapidly accumulating beach constantly thrown up by the Gulf Stream, which rushes past between Cape Florida and the Bimini Islands with a velocity of six or seven miles an hour. After heavy rains, the beach is broken through, and the waters mingle with the sea, but in general they form large lagoons lying parallel to the coast.

Indian River is a beautiful sheet of water or lagoon, formed in this manner by the waters of the many streams, extending upwards of 100 miles along the coast, with a narrow inlet scarcely 20 yards across, and only four or five feet water on the bar.

Mosquito Lagoon lies immediately North of Indian River, separated by a long narrow isthmus, scarcely a quarter of a mile in breadth.

Nassau River collects all the waters between the St. John's and St. Mary's Rivers, and discharges them about midway between their mouths.

St. Mary's River forms the boundary between Florida and Georgia. Until within these few years it was always supposed to originate in the Oke-fin-o-cau Swamp, but recent surveys have satisfactorily proved that this is not the case. The source of the St. Mary's River is in latitude 30° 35' North, longitude 82° 17' West, and the mouth between Amelia and Cumberland Islands, in latitude 30° 48' North, longitude 81° 37' West. The length of its course, which is very circuitous, is nearly 100 miles.

Some of the Florida rivers which pass through the lime-stone country have natural bridges spanning the stream, where it has forced its way through some original fissures in the rock. The Santaffy has several such; and in one place is said to run subterraneously for two miles. But no authentic account has yet been obtained on this head.

The lakes are numerous. *Lake George* and *Lake Macaco* are the principal.

There is no good Harbour on the Eastern coast of Florida, except that formed by the mouth of St. Mary's River, which affords entrance to vessels drawing 22 feet water. The Harbour of Key West, on the Florida reef, is good, but difficult of approach. Charlotte Harbour and Tampa Bay have both very excellent anchorage, and all quite landlocked. St. George's Sound, within Appalachia Bay, will hereafter become a place of resort for shipping, and the Harbour of Pensacola has long been well known.

The Civil divisions have not become sufficiently permanent to be recorded; and it is highly probable that the portion of West Florida adjacent to Alabama will shortly be annexed to that State. At the time of the cession to the United States the population of East Florida did not exceed 3000; that of West Florida might perhaps have amounted to 1500; and the small remnant of Indian population to 1000 or 1200. The greatest number of inhabitants was therefore barely 6000. Since 1821 this number has probably increased, and if the total is assumed to be at present 10,000, it will probably be nearly just.

The chief, in fact the only, Towns of Florida, are St. Augustine, Pensacola, and Fernandina. Various others have been laid out lately, particularly Talahassee, the new Capital; but as yet the woods on which it is to be built are scarcely felled.

St. Augustine, the Capital of East Florida, was built in 1565, and is undoubtedly the oldest Town on the American continent, except those on the Mexican settlements. In 1763 some of the original houses remained with the date 1571 upon the front, and all were without chimnies or glazed windows. Sir Francis Drake pillaged the Town in 1586, as did the Indians in 1611, and Captain Davis in 1665. St. Augustine was besieged unsuccessfully by the British Colonists in 1702, in 1725, and in 1740, and likewise by the Insurgents in 1813. Its preservation was owing to the Fortress of St. Marc, a regular square fortification with bastions, built of the shell stone of the country. So costly have been the outlays on this fort, that the late King of Spain once inquired whether it was built of gold.

St. Augustine is situated on a neck of land formed by its own Harbour and a tributary creek, with the Island of Anastatia between the Town and the sea. It is regularly laid out, forming a parallelogram somewhat more than a quarter of a mile from East to West, and three quarters of a mile from North to South. The streets are narrow; the houses next the Harbour are built of the shell stone found in the quarries on Anastatia Island, with only one story above the ground floor; these latter are invariably laid with a layer of *tabbia*, a mixture of sand and pounded shells, and are used for store rooms, &c., the families living in the upper story. The dwellings of the poorer kind are built of wood with *tabbia* floors. St. Augustine has long been celebrated as the Montpelier of North America. In 1784, when re-ceded to Spain, the beauty and high order of the gardens, the neatness of the houses, and the air of comfort and cheerfulness every where around, were the admiration of the invalids and other strangers who resorted hither. Neglect and consequent decay attended this interesting Town during its occupancy by the Spaniards; and in 1821 it appeared ruinous, dirty and forbidding. The houses built of wood are not so eligible for a residence in this Town as those constructed with the shell rock. This remarkable formation consists of deep beds of small indurated bivalve shells, cemented together either by original pressure, or the gluten from the gristle of the hinge of the shells, which are often detached unbroken. When quarried, the rock is soft, but it hardens by exposure to the atmosphere. It is found all along the coast as far as Cape Florida, and appears in a few places on the Island of Cuba, and then is no more known. The population of St. Augustine in 1821 was about 1500. At present the number of inhabitants are nearly 3000. Latitude 29° 51' North, longitude 81° 27' West of Greenwich. Distant 316 miles South-West from Charleston in South Carolina, and 240 from the entrance of the Gulf of Florida.

Pensacola, the Capital of West Florida, appears to have been founded sometime previous to 1696. It was frequently taken and retaken by the French and Spaniards, and was finally restored to Spain in 1722. The prosperity and decay of Pensacola seem to have been similar to those of its sister City. The population in 1821 was about 1000; at present it is nearly doubled. Latitude 30° 35' North, longitude 87° 13' West of Greenwich.

At the North end of Amelia Island is the small Town of *Fernandina*, which sprang up during the American embargo in 1808 and the subsequent war; the excellence of its anchorage, and its proximity to St. Mary's, made it the resort of the vessels who came to procure the Georgia cotton which was smuggled across the river. The population was not more than 500 in 1821. Its geographical position is that of the mouth of the river St. Mary before-mentioned.

A small village has been erected under the walls of Fort *St. Marc*, near the head of Appalachia Bay, and on the river of that name. It is little more than a military post. Latitude 30° 12' North, longitude 84° 11' West.

Micampy is a new Town in the heart of the country.

Many Towns have been built in Florida, and abandoned in consequence of political and other changes. *New Smyrna*, or *Mosquito*, is one of them; and remains of settlements and villages made by the Spaniards in the XVIIth century are found in many places, but their records are lost.

The Indians were formerly very numerous in the Floridas, probably as much so as in Mexico; the histories of the earliest travellers assure us of this fact, and the vestiges remaining to the present day attest it. From various causes, however, they have gradually, and within the last 40 years rapidly, disappeared, particularly from East Florida; and the once numerous Tribes are now reduced to a few bands of indolent, dirty vagabonds, the broken remnants of the Seminola Tribes and refugees from the Creeks and Choctaws, and some few of the Euchees. This impoverished remainder of the aboriginal inhabitants is about to be concentrated in one part of Florida, and in a few years probably will be extinct.

The general Florida reef commences at Cape Florida on the Eastern coast, in latitude 25° 38' North, and trends away about

South-West to Bay Honda, 25 or 30 miles South of Cape Sable, whence it sweeps nearly West, until terminated by the Tortugas Bank. The edge of soundings, which are chiefly 100 fathoms, is nearly parallel to the outer edge of the reef; within which, between the banks and the Keys or islets, is a channel with about 15 feet of water.

The *Keys* are numerous small islands lying within the great reef, and frequented by navigators who earn their livelihood by watching for the vessels which the tempests prevalent in the Gulf Stream drive on to the shoals; these are chiefly heavy laden European ships, laden with colonial produce, and the salvage on their cargoes pays the speculating wreckers, who are generally inhabitants of the Bahama Islands. The Keys were the great rendezvous for the piratical cruisers so prevalent on this coast some years since, and also formed a safe retreat for the Buccaneers of old. Very few of the Keys are fit for cultivation. *Key Largo*, which in fact is a long peninsula attached to the main land of Florida, was formerly abundant in mastic, lignum vitae, and logwood, which have long since been cut down. Upon *Old Maticombe Key* are some fine natural wells of fresh water in the solid rock, which are well known to the pilots on the coast. The ship-wrecked crew of a large French Indiaman, 300 in number, was destroyed here formerly by the Coloosas Indians, a Tribe now extinct.

The most important of the group is an island called by the Spaniards *Cayo Huesso*, (*Bone Key*,) and by the English *Key West*; since the cession it has been named *Thompson's Island*. Key West extends six or seven miles East and West, being two miles wide at most; the West point is fertile, and contains fresh water pools and wells; the Eastern half is barren. The Island abounds in natural salt ponds, generally allowed to be of the very best kind; and sufficient, if properly managed, to supply all North America with salt. It is remarkable that no salt ponds exist in any other of the Keys. Key West possesses a good anchorage, ground or roadsteed, with 24 feet water. Hence to the Havanna the distance is only 25 leagues.

Among the long catalogue of fishes which haunt the Florida Keys, are turtle and a remarkable species of prawn, found in the holes of the coral rocks, beautifully spotted with red, yellow, green, gray, and black, and of the size of a lobster.

Key Tavernier is the principal resort of the wreckers. The duties to the British Government, collected at Nassau upon sales of property recovered by these people from vessels wrecked on the reef, produced £15,000 annually.

The works best worth attention on Florida are *La Florida del Ynca, Historia del adelantado Hernando Soto, escrita por el Ynca,* Garcilasso de la Vega, 1591, (edition in 4to, *en Lisboa,* 1605;) in French by Richelet, Leyden, 1726; *Relation of the Invasion and Conquest of Florida by the Spaniards under Fernando de Soto,* by a Portuguese Gentleman of Elvas, in 1539, London, 8vo, 1686, from a rare and curious Manuscript; *De Gallorum in Floridam expeditione, et insigni Hispanorum in eos saevitiae exemplo. Brevis Historia,* (appended to Benzoni's work on the *New World,* entitled *Novae Novi Orbis Historiae,* Genevae, 1578, 8vo, and given in Calveton's translation in French, as *Vne petite Histoire d'vn Massacre commis par les Hespagnols sur quelques Francois en la Floride,* Geneva, 1579;) *Historia General de Yndias, por* Herrera, 4 vols. folio, (Madrid edition, 1730;) *Histoire Naturelle et Morale des Iles Antilles de l'Amerique, par* Rochefort, second edition, 4to, Rotterdam, 1665, in which is a long and very interesting account of the ancient Floridians; *A Relation of a Discovery lately made on the coast of Florida* by William Hilton, *giving an Account of the Nature and Temperament of the Soil, the Manners and Disposition of the Natives, and whatsoever else is remarkable therein; together with Proposals made by the Commissioners of the Lords Proprietors to all such Persons as shall become the first Settlers on the Rivers, Harbours, and Creeks there,* London, 1664, 4to; Purchas, *Pilgrims,* vol. iii. p. 807, vol. iv. p. 1532, and vol. iv.; *Virginia richly valued, by the Description of the Maine Land of Florida, her next neighbor,* 4to, *Dat. from my lodging in the Colledge of Westminster,* 15 *Ap.* 1609, Richard Hakluyt, (this is a translation from the Portuguese of the second work we have mentioned, and is now very scarce;) Book viii. of Purchas *his Pilgrimes* also contains a collection of Voyages to Virginia and Florida, London, 1625; Hakluyt, p. 543 and p. 679; *The Generall Historie of Virginia, New England, and the Summer Isles, from their first beginning Anno* 1584 *to the present* 1626, *by* Captain John Smith, *sometime Governor in those Countries and Admiral of New England,* London, folio, 1627; *Historiae Indiae Occidentalis* Hieronymo Benzone Italo et Joanne Lerio Burgundo, *testibus oculatis autoribus,* Urbani Calvetonis et G. M. Studio, *conversi,* 1636, 8vo; *A Description of the English Province of Carolana, by the Spaniards called Florida, and by the French La Louisiane*, &c. by Daniel Coxe, London, 8vo, 1727; Cardenas, *Ensayo Cronologico para la Historia General de la Florida*, Madrid, folio, 1733; Bartram and Stock's *East Florida*, 4to, London, 1769; Roberts and Jeffrey's *First Discovery and Natural History of Florida*, 4to, London, 1763; Bartram's *Travels in East and West Florida*, &c. *in* 1773, 8vo, London; Catesby's *Natural History of Carolina, Florida, and the Bahama Islands*, by Edwards, 2 vols. folio, London, 1771; Alcedo, *Geographical and Historical Dictionary of America*, by Thompson, 5 vols. 4to, London, 1810; Robin, *Voyage dans l'intérieure de la Floride Occidentale*, &c. 1802–1806, 3 vols. Paris; Touron, *Histoire Générale de l'Amérique depuis sa Découverte*, 14 vols. Paris, 1768–1770; Major Stoddart's *Louisiana;* and Carey and Lea's *American Atlas*, give some recent but limited accounts of this Country. A good modern Geographical, Natural History, and Statistical account, is a primary want amongst the many other desiderata on the subject of South America.

INDEX.